Unique Common Sense Strategies for Children with Sensory and Regulation Challenges

NO LONGER A

SECRET *Second Edition*

Lucy Jane Miller, PhD, OTR

Lisa M. Porter, PhD, PTD, OTR/L

Doreit S. Bialer, OTD, MA, OTR

No Longer A SECRET, Second Edition

All marketing and publishing rights guaranteed to and reserved by:

Phone: 817-277-0727 or 800-489-0727 (toll-free)

Fax: 817-277-2270

www.sensoryworld.com

ISBN: 9781949177688

DEDICATION

I dedicate this book to both of my children, Arianna Rachel and Alec Ross. You both inspire me to continue my journey in helping children and families with Sensory Processing Disorder. Many special thanks to my sister, Zipora, and to my mom, for your unconditional love and support, and to Annie, Anthony, and Keri for believing in me.

— D. S. B.

To the children, mothers, and fathers, and siblings who have been my "professors" on this journey to understanding Sensory Processing Disorder. Special thanks to the staff and faculty at the STAR Institute, and to my own sensational family. None of this would have happened without your generosity and dedication, above and beyond what anyone could expect. It does, after all, take a village to provide hope and help to children with SPD and their families.

— L. J. M.

A SECRET is a labor of love for me, and I am grateful for the opportunity to make this tool more widely available for individuals with sensory processing differences. I dedicate this book to all of the children, families, and mentees who have brainstormed with me over the years to create dynamic and individualized sensory lifestyles using A SECRET. I am grateful to the families who participated in my dissertation study, offering invaluable reflections on their experiences with A SECRET. Lastly, I extend a special thanks to "Luke" and his family who flourished with A SECRET and allowed me to be a part of their team in a deep and connected way.

— L. M. P.

PREFACE TO THE SECOND EDITION

What happens when something feels bad but you don't know what's wrong with you? How are you supposed to feel when your condition has been diagnosed, then re-diagnosed, and you don't understand any of it? Where do you go when you feel lost and confused, when no one believes you and not even your parents know what to do?

As a teenager, I had a serious problem. I was losing my eyesight, and no one could figure out why. I could see with my contact lenses, but when I took them out, images were fuzzy and diffuse. Things got worse over time, and by age 15, I could barely detect anything except light and dark without my contacts. The lenses hurt my eyes, and I'd often blink one out and have to spend hours on my hands and knees trying to find it. I'd had a happy childhood until I "went weird" as a teenager.

My parents—both loving, educated professionals—took me to an ophthalmologist, who said there was nothing wrong with my eyes. "It's all in her head," he said. On some level, pretty much everyone suspected I was making up the blurriness, the pain of wearing contacts—the whole deal. My pediatrician and school nurse were sure I'd scripted this teen-age drama to get attention. My high-school guidance counselor knew about this psychiatric issue of Lucy "making things up" and advised me not to apply to a top-tier college, saying, "Go where you know you'll be accepted, Lucy, or you may not get in at all."

Even I, myself, began to wonder what could be so wrong in my head that I was imagining all these eye issues. I thought maybe I was crazy. And if I were, what could I do about it? I was still a child. Where could I turn? In that era, the 1960s, *psychiatrist* was a word that conjured thoughts of mental institutions, shock therapy, and people roaming the grounds, foaming at the mouth. I felt alone with my fuzzy vision and fears.

What happened next is laid out in my first book, *Sensational Kids*, but what's key to the book you're reading now are two painful memories. One was that *people didn't believe me*. To this day, that has affected and shaped my life. The other was that my sensations *weren't like* those of my friends. Although I saw less, I heard much more (my children claim I can hear through walls!) And I *felt* more, both through my fingertips and through my heart and soul. This became apparent in my early 20s, when I finally received a diagnosis of keratoconus and was treated by receiving corneal transplants. After the transplant surgeries, both my eyes were patched for six months, and I wasn't allowed to move my body or head. During that time, I noticed that when somebody walked into my room, I'd know immediately how the person felt, even if the person was a stranger. As "woo-woo" as that may seem, it's true. As palpably as if I used any sight, sound, or smell, I could tell if a person was happy, angry, embarrassed, or whatever. I could sense how people were feeling.

This intense awareness of my own shifting sensory boundaries prompted me to spend the next 35 years studying children's sensory systems and trying to help parents and siblings understand *sensational* kids. In many ways, my work—like that of many professionals in the "helping" professions—is an attempt to work out the frustrations and anxieties I experienced during my own youth.

PREFACE TO THE SECOND EDITION

Sensory Processing Disorder (SPD) has gained significant ground since the first edition of this book was published. Ongoing research continues to diminish the stigma associated with this *invisible* disorder (and the gaslighting that I experienced as a teenager). Thanks in large part to the SPD scientific work group, funded by the Wallace Foundation, researchers from multiple disciplines, including occupational therapy, have greatly improved our understanding of SPD. At the same time, global awareness of sensory disorders continues to grow, generating a new initiative for overall sensory health and wellness. You don't need to have a "disorder" to benefit from strategies to support sensory health and wellness! The more we know about our own sensory differences, the more resilient and better able we are to support our kids with SPD. Of course, we still have a long way to go. There is always more work to be done and more questions to ask.

So, what now? We must work locally and globally to build our awareness so that all people—children and adults alike—who struggle with sensory processing differences get what they need to cope: early identification, assessment, and treatment, if needed. That includes understanding how to provide supports in varied contexts.

The first edition of this book was a follow-up to *Sensational Kids*, which tells the story of five children with SPD as they proceed through a typical day. *Sensational Kids* explains the subtypes of SPD in a way that readers can relate to and understand. Although it touches on treatment, there isn't enough space to really dive into intervention or strategies. SPD is a complex disorder, and no single strategy works for everyone. This book takes on the challenge of addressing dynamic supports to help families create a sensory lifestyle and meet individual needs.

Every child is unique, with individual sensory differences, regulation needs, and most importantly, distinct relationships with family, friends, and community. Over the years, we have come to realize the essential role of relationships in supporting children with SPD. As therapists, parents, teachers, and caregivers, we must learn to attune to our children. We need to recognize their individual sensory and regulatory needs. Yes, we will always provide sensory tools and supports, but it is relationships that provide children the tools to develop emotion-regulation or self-regulation skills.

In this book, you will see a definite shift in focus. We are no longer emphasizing SPD subtypes, because the strategies discussed in each element of A SECRET are not bound by subtypes. We realized that the focus on subtypes forced limits on using the tools and strategies by almost putting them in a box. A SECRET is the opposite of a box! It is a dynamic and ever-changing framework that allows us to identify supports for our children (and families) regardless of the setting or context. When we learn to use this framework, we can use the strategies in each element of A SECRET to support our children at any moment.

One big change in this edition is the shift from *Attention to Attunement*. This element emphasizes individual differences and the important focus on regulation. Instead of rigidly holding on to the idea that a child fits into any one (or two or three) SPD subtype, we need to attune (observe, recognize, attend) to their cues, looking for changes in regulation. This means first attuning to ourselves! As caregivers, we are the best tool we have. When we attune to our own regulation, we are better able to attune to and co-regulate our children (much more on this in chapters 3 and 5)!

After years of observing, consulting, and running the mentorship program for experienced therapists at the STAR Institute (co-directed by Dr. Sarah A. Schoen and now the STAR faculty), I'm well aware of therapists trained in a traditional model of treating sensory issues who may be feeling dissatisfied and "stuck." Having been trained and mentored by Dr. A. Jean Ayres, I, too, used her treatment model for decades. In fact, the randomized clinical trial that my colleagues and I published in 2007 was a 15-year culmination of research that provided empirical evidence for the validity of this approach. The Ayres Sensory Integration treatment approach is an incredibly valuable and effective component of our approach at STAR, and I've become convinced that other aspects of intervention are equally important. Regulating a child's arousal levels, for example, deserves more emphasis in treatment. So, too, do elements of relationship and engagement, and certainly fostering parent education and coaching. This book includes elements of each of these essential components of intervention.

During her mentorship program at the STAR Institute, Doreit Bialer asked for my feedback on an early version of the first edition of *No Longer A SECRET*. Her approaches appealed to me. I loved the idea of implementing low-cost, low-tech strategies for children with sensorimotor issues. I also wanted to help a wider audience understand the underlying principles that trained experts use to treat their young clients and to help them learn to problem-solve on their own.

Lisa Porter has been my mentee since 2009, when she started the intensive mentorship program at STAR. Since then, she has worked with me and the other faculty members at STAR to grow and develop the mentorship program. Lisa's dissertation research involved using A SECRET as the foundation of group parent-training to help caregivers problem-solve supports for their children and families. Given Lisa's experience with A SECRET, it made perfect sense to ask her to join us in writing this edition of *No Longer A SECRET*.

In Doreit and Lisa, I discovered open-minded and enthusiastic partners who were excited about the process of collaborating and brainstorming to find the best possible way to present this framework.

Together, we've written this book for you, highlighting what we've learned collectively over the years. At times, we speak directly to you, the parents. Other times, we speak to you, the teachers. And at some points, we speak to you, the therapists. We all have so much to learn. I often say, "The kids are *my* professors." When a child is particularly complex or puzzling, the child becomes our best teacher of all. We must continue to grow by asking questions every day.

Though the research is ever-evolving, I do know this much for certain: SPD is not a reflection of bad behavior, and it is not caused by bad parenting. In fact, it's not "bad" at all. It's physiologic in nature.

If you are worried that your child might have SPD, take the first step and get an evaluation done by a multidisciplinary team. (For more information on multidisciplinary evaluations, go to *www.sensoryhealth. org*). You can also join (or start) your local SPD Parent Connections group. The earlier SPD is identified, the earlier a child will learn to cope with it. And the sooner parents learn A SECRET when it comes to helping their child, the sooner stresses will ease in the whole family. I do not mean that parents should become therapists. Instead, families should be taught the *principles* of therapy rather than just trying to follow their therapist's suggestions. Then families and therapists can work together to embed therapeutic interventions into the natural days of children who are receiving treatment.

We hope this book gives you a framework for strategies to use the next time you need them. There is help. There is hope. We're all in this together. And believe me: no matter the doubts of the medical orthodoxy, there are a lot of us.

— Dr. Lucy Jane Miller
May 2021

PREFACE: DOREIT'S STORY

It wasn't until I adopted my first child that I'd ever loved anyone so intensely that no words could describe the feeling. I remember the phone call we got to congratulate my husband and me for being the "new adoptive parents" of our son, born in February 1995. We were both so overjoyed, we screamed and cried—it was a mixture of a thousand emotions that had been pent up for so long.

Our precious boy, Alec Ross, awaited our arrival 9 days after his birth. The delay in bringing him home from the hospital stemmed from "a couple of minor concerns"—he was jaundiced and had a small head. Still, we were assured that he was perfect. My best friend at the time, a neonatologist, carefully read all the medical reports and asked if we were sure we wanted to go through with this particular adoption. "Are you kidding?" my husband and I answered. "Of course!" And so we began our personal education in Sensory Processing Disorder (SPD).

Our son came home from the hospital with projectile vomiting and severe irritability. Among many distressing behaviors, Alec fought against being held and kissed. As a new mom, I was at once madly in love but stressed out and confused. By the time he was 15 days old, I'd arranged for an early-intervention team to start evaluating our son, who cried throughout their assessment. After what seemed like a lifetime, the therapists left and came back with a caseworker within a week's time. My husband and I were presented with a long list of our son's problems. My mind wandered as I blocked out the therapists' presentation. It sounded like a lot of noise to me. Their words were impersonal and offered no solutions—the team just went through a long list of worries that seemed to rationalize the need for each of their intensive intervention services. In all their chatter, I remember looking down at my sleeping baby and thinking, "These people don't really know you." And you know what? I was right.

That team of professionals, confabbing in our living room 16 years ago, knew nothing at all about Alec Ross. They knew nothing about how well he would ice skate at age 5 or how much he'd love tinkering with engines when he was 11. They had no idea how creative and artistic he would become.They couldn't predict how easily he'd be able to say "I love you" as a teenager, and really mean it. And they couldn't have known that he would grow up to be one of the most tender young men on the planet. To them, Alec was just a cluster of challenges and symptoms. Still, we needed their help. "Thank you all," I remember telling the therapists, as they handed me a long list of expensive therapy equipment to buy and a schedule of dates and times they'd be coming back to work with my son.

Until you experience being the parent of a child with SPD, you can't really understand the desperation of wanting to help, the vulnerability to experts' advice, and the willingness to do whatever is necessary at whatever cost—even if it means turning your warm and cozy home into a therapy clinic. No treatment is too expensive, no intervention is too time-consuming, and no doctor's office is too far if it means potentially sparing your child the negative feedback, social awkwardness, name-calling, isolation, confusion, and low self-esteem that come with

SPD. What's essential is to remember who your sensational child is, beyond labels and diagnoses. He or she has beautiful and amazing talents that maybe only you get to see. Alec is not only a kid with sensory craving and dyspraxia. He's a smart, funny, polite, talented, personable, charming, and passionate 16-year-old who has lots of dreams that keep him going. Always knowing that—even during the loudest tantrums and toughest meltdowns—has helped our family navigate our way through it.

Professionally, my education in SPD started 15 years into my career as an occupational therapist, when the school where I was working asked me to greet students at the bus every morning. Immediately, I noticed remarkable differences in the way the children got off the bus. Some kids jumped down the stairs and skipped to the classroom, where they eagerly unpacked their belongings and got ready to start their day. Others had to be carried off the bus, screaming and kicking. It was clear that these differences seemed to reflect more than the kids' attitudes about school. The bus ride itself, I realized, could be overwhelming. The bumps and noises, the stops and starts, the close contact with other kids, and the invasion of personal space could be completely overloading and disorganizing to some children.Why, I wondered, could some kids cope on the bus, while others fell apart?

As it turned out, many of the kids who had trouble staying seated on their 30-minute ride to school also couldn't sit still during math lessons. It wasn't a coincidence that the first-grader who found the bus ride too noisy in the mornings cowered from the drumming in music class each afternoon. And it was no wonder that the third-grader who panicked whenever anyone opened a window on the bus also lost concentration when his teacher turned on a fan to cool down the classroom. Children like these were clearly experiencing sensory input differently than their schoolmates. They were demonstrating signs of SPD—the patterns were obvious.

My personal experiences with my son and professional experiences in helping students cope with their own sensory challenges led me to devise strategies and low-cost tools to assist kids with SPD. In time, I came to learn that kids don't need fancy therapy equipment or brand names to deal with sensorimotor challenges. Just as nobody's jump shot improves by buying a pair of LeBron James Nikes, the nervous system doesn't care what brand of therapy equipment you use or how much it costs.

In the schools where I worked, special services never had the budgets to buy much gear at all. It was up to me to bring my own equipment to treat children who qualified for occupational-therapy services. The more my caseload grew, the more I bought. Eventually, I lugged my menagerie of equipment to school each day in a rolling suitcase. Soon, my role as an occupational therapist began to change as teachers asked for more and more help in the classroom. It became unrealistic to walk up and down flights of stairs with a heavy Samsonite. Besides, students were facing so many different issues in each classroom that the concept of "one size fits all" wasn't going to work.

That's when I started making individualized, low-tech objects for each child. This required spontaneity and creativity in using items readily available in the classroom. My favorite ones included a 2-inch loose-leaf binder, enlarged rubber bands, masking tape, and students' own jackets and sweaters. With these, I found ways of developing substitutes for therapeutic items, including wedges for posture, slant boards, sitting disks, bolsters, balance boards, weighted vests, compression jackets, and even suspended equipment. I realized that my students didn't recognize the differences or care about whether we were using expensive, "state-of-the-art" equipment from the glossy catalogues. In fact, most of the kids beyond first grade were happy to learn strategies based on materials that didn't look different or "weird."

Remembering how important it is to establish relationships and trust with kids, I got so adept at making positive changes without all the fancy stuff that I finally left my suitcase behind. When the economy faltered in 2008, using everyday objects became even more imperative to the families of students, to the schools, and to my own practice. I let everyone know that we would figure out how to meet each child's needs by making our own substitutes to replace pricy, brand-named equipment.

In 2010, I registered for an intensive mentorship program at the Sensory Processing Disorder Foundation in Colorado, which was taught by Dr Lucy Jane Miller, Dr Sarah Schoen, and staff members of the Sensory Therapies And Research (STAR) Center, which Dr Miller directs. It was a life-changing experience. I shared my ideas with Dr Miller, and we decided to coauthor this book to build on my experiences with low-cost, low-tech strategies to help children with SPD. Writing this book has been a meaningful journey for me, and one that I hope you will learn from. Most of all, I want to convey hope to all parents—that you can help your kids by using thoughtful strategies that do not involve expensive, technologically sophisticated equipment. As Dr Miller always says, "The best tool you have to help a child with SPD is *you!*"

We urge you to review the chapters in consecutive order and not skip around on the assumption that one particular subtype of SPD pertains to your child. Children with SPD usually don't fit neatly into a single classification. They typically demonstrate behaviors indicative of issues in more than one subtype. So please stay with it—all of it. Take the time to learn about all of the many aspects of the disorder—the subtypes and the symptoms. Learn how to use Dr Miller's strategic approach, which she dubs "A SECRET." SPD treatment does not need to be perplexing and expensive any longer.

— Doreit Sarah Bialer
April 2011

REFLECTIONS FROM LISA

I've been working with and learning from Dr. Miller for over a decade. Over the years, she's helped me progress from a novice in SPD to a skilled clinician, then a mentor, then finally, a researcher. I am grateful for all I've learned—and continue to learn—from Dr. Miller and for this opportunity to further develop A SECRET with her.

I've been using and teaching A SECRET since I participated in the STAR Level 1 Intensive Mentorship Program in 2009. I am incredibly grateful for the knowledge I received from my mentor at STAR, Jamie Schreckler (a former STAR therapist and faculty member). Jamie is a master at what she identified as "process points," or individualized supportive strategies that are the magic of A SECRET. I worked alongside Jamie and Dr. Miller to adapt and improve A SECRET for our parents and mentees. After years of using this framework with parents, kids, and therapists, I decided it was time to dig deeper. I love A SECRET! I love seeing how it empowers families, especially how it can shift their perspectives. Using A SECRET allows parents to realize that they can support their children in almost any situation. Using this framework as a starting point, kids and families learn to use their strengths to support their challenge areas across many different contexts.

As amazing as A SECRET can be, I've also seen parents at their wit's end, too stressed to take in so much information. It can be overwhelming to look at all of the different elements and think about where strategies fit into the framework. This overwhelmingness led me to ask questions. Thanks to Dr. Miller's mentoring, I have been conditioned to ask questions and to do my best to answer them. So I had to find out more. How can we best use A SECRET to help parents learn? How can we adapt it to fit parents who don't have time, energy, or resources to use A SECRET to problem-solve the answers to different challenges? And what about the parents who do have the support systems and resources to dive deeper, parents who might have been living in this SPD world for years and are ready to learn more? How can we use this tool, this framework, to meet the needs of kids and families at different levels of stress, understanding, resilience, and readiness to change? To answer these questions, I wanted to hear parents' voices, not just rely on my own experience. So I decided to design my dissertation research around answering these questions!

Along with Breanne Kearney, one of the passionate and dedicated occupational therapists (OTs) at my clinic, I designed a series of workshops to teach parents about A SECRET and about how to use it to support their children. Bre and I spent months gathering and analyzing data on parents' perceptions of A SECRET. How did they take in information about the tool? What did they learn from the process? What did they take away when they hardly had time to attend the workshops, much less try to find the energy to problem-solve in the moment?

We found that A SECRET can be an excellent tool for parents across a dynamic spectrum of readiness for information. It is easily adaptable to meet many different needs. It can be as individual as our kids and as unique as the families we see in our clinics. My research indicated that for some parents, A SECRET was life-changing. It allowed them to begin to understand the complexities of SPD and their children. With this understanding, they were able to shift their perspectives on the behaviors they were seeing. They realized that they had many ways to support their children in varied contexts and learned to problem-solve in the moment.

For other parents, it was overwhelming and too much information to think about the big picture of A SECRET. Let's face it: parenting is exhausting! Especially when you are challenged with the behaviors that can come with SPD. Even parents who found the information overwhelming walked away with new strategies and a new understanding of themselves and their children. These parents reported that A SECRET was helpful in organizing the strategies and suggestions that they received in the workshops or from their child's therapist. Many reported taking away specific strategies without having to use all of the categories of A SECRET. They said that the tangible suggestions (that we cover later in this book) were the critical pieces for them. But it wasn't just about the strategies; in every case, these parents also reported thinking differently about their interactions with their child, which helped them stay regulated in stressful moments. As you will read in Chapter 3, these calm interactions are at least as essential as the sensory strategies or environmental adaptations you might make to support your child.

I am grateful to the parents who participated in my research and to all of the families who have problem-solved with me over the years. Your participation helps us learn so much more about using A SECRET. I hope to spend many more years learning from and problem-solving with families, and I know A SECRET will be a part of that learning. I hope this second edition of *No Longer A SECRET* will help create a learning and problem-solving culture for families and individuals with SPD.

CHAPTER 1

INTRODUCTION

What Is the Big Secret? Kris' Story

Mrs. Anderson sat in the observation room with me, Dr. Miller, looking through the one-way mirror into the occupational therapy (OT) treatment room. She said:

"Well, I can see how well he does with your therapist, Renee. That's because she's an OT, and all you OTs know the secrets of how to make kids behave. I'm just his mom, and although I'm a good lawyer, I don't know your OT secrets. He would never do the things we are looking at now."

I looked at her incredulously. And that's when it began to sink into my mind. **SECRET?** What is a secret and why does she think we occupational therapists (OTs) have secrets?

When you talk about A SECRET, what is the secret? I looked up "secret" in the dictionary. It said:

> "A secret is done, made, or conducted without the knowledge
> of others, such as parents or teachers. To be entrusted with
> a secret, a person must work to escape notice, knowledge, or
> observation, e.g., a secret drawer, the secret police."

But as OTs, we don't want to keep the knowledge away from others. It is not just the initiated or privileged who are allowed to understand the methods used. We are not practicing magic (although it may seem like it sometimes)!

A person can be said to keep a secret if they are close-mouthed: unwilling to tell what they know, cautious in keeping what they do know confidential (or, in other words, reticent to tell parents and teachers what the process and activities are really doing for the client). When teachers and parents understand the purpose of the activity, they become a valuable member of the team. Our goal is to give more information to the players on the team.

The secret of OT is this: OT *does* work for improving many things. It *is* effective in helping children and their parents[1] experience change. But the effectiveness is limited by the ability of the parent to articulate and understand specific goals and strategies. And that means that the parent/teacher must be focused on the most important big-picture factors that are interfering with the child's ability to move forward. What

---

1. In this book, we are using the term 'parents' to make the book more readable, but that word is meant to include all caregivers of the child (parents, grandparents, significant others, etc.)

we mean by move forward is not a developmental increase in motor skills or sensory-motor ability, but rather an improvement in social factors such as participation and relationships.

We believe that the focus for any client must be on that which brings **joy** and **success** to the parent/teacher and the child rather than that which brings small and ultimately non-important developmental steps or specific skills such as improving pencil grasp, balancing on one foot, or tying her shoes. This is further explained in the two examples below.

In the example referenced above, Mr. and Mrs. Anderson had been in OT previously. When questioned about Kris' goals, they listed almost 20. At least they had a good idea of what goals their OT had for Kris! The problem was those goals were not functional. Let's say the OT's goal was improving muscle tone; how would the parents know when this had been achieved? There were so many goals for Kris, and the parents didn't understand the functional implications of these goals, so they felt he wasn't making progress.

The OT had given the parents bits and pieces of information, which the parents learned were the basic factors contributing to their child's challenges. They had learned highly technical words that they did not truly understand. The Andersons were with us for a short-term, intensive (daily) treatment. In two weeks, we were to reevaluate Kris and get an idea of what a meaningful treatment program would be for little Kris so that his parents could make sure he got these meaningful features when he went home. This is hard, because two weeks is a short time to form a solid bond with a parent or child, but we have found it to be a useful way to begin getting parents to formulate a reasonable path. Also, many families do return at a later date or at least know to seek a relationship-based sensory therapist at home.

The Andersons had tracked me down on day three of treatment, clearly agitated. "Can we talk to you?" they asked. "Of course," I replied, and I knew better than to keep them waiting. I found a small parent education/consult room that was free, and we sat down.

MRS. ANDERSON: We are very upset because your OT is not doing what she is supposed to do.

ME: Really? Tell me more about this. What is Kris' therapist supposed to do?

MRS. ANDERSON: Well, Kris has cerebellar dysfunction. He needs proprioceptive and vestibular stimulation to fix it.

ME: Okay, I see you have been trained before or read things on the web or in books.

MRS. ANDERSON: Yes, that's the way I learn. We try to read and understand everything that can help us be the best parents we can be.

ME: Right, I get it, and I applaud you for your efforts. Tell me this: how will you know when his cerebellar issues are better? What kind of changes are you looking for?

MRS. ANDERSON: That's obvious, isn't it? (*I didn't think so.*) His vestibular and proprioceptive functioning will improve.

ME: (*I wanted to tread softly but still communicate with Mrs. Anderson.*) I assume you know what proprioceptive and vestibular input looks like, but do you know what it is hypothesized to do?

MRS. ANDERSON: I think I understand it. The vestibular sense tells us where our heads are in space, especially related to 'gravity'? Actually, I'm not entirely sure what that means, but I know I've read it. Vestibular is like ... am I standing up or lying down, and the movement of my brain up and down stimulates receptors that process movement sensation and begin to lay down a map in the brain. This is how typically developing children can tell where their bodies are in space. And the proprioceptive sense tells us how one or a few other parts of our bodies are related to other parts of our body, like is my arm in front of or behind my body?

ME: Right! I can see you've been studying this. But did anything you read tell you how vestibular and proprioceptive input could affect the cerebellum? And what indicated that Kris had a cerebellar dysfunction?

MRS. ANDERSON: (*She was beginning to see the light.*) I see what you are getting at. But if he doesn't have a cerebellar problem, what does he have?

ME: That's an important and complex question, one we are trying to answer or at least answer in part with our evaluation. Can we take a step back?

MRS. ANDERSON: Sure. Let's do that.

ME: Let's go back to the basic question here. What things do you hope to see change—not proprioceptive or vestibular symptoms, but maybe behaviors related to social participation, self-esteem and self-regulation? What are Kris' most important issues?

(*Mrs. Anderson looked blank. I prompted her.*)

What concerns are you having at home? Does he throw a temper tantrum if he doesn't get his way? What self-care skills get in the way of his success at home or at school? Or...? Ultimately, what are your hopes for therapy outcomes? Making and keeping friends? Joining the family at dinner? Having meaningful relationships?

Our conversation went on from there, and we began to get on the same page. Did this take time? You bet it did. Was it worth it? It was— it certainly was! I was not trying to convince Mrs. Anderson that she was wrong. I wasn't trying to say, "Listen to me, I'm right and you are wrong." I was gently trying to bring Mrs. Anderson into my process of thinking without implying that she was wrong.

A truly skilled therapist understands that they are not always right and don't have to have all the answers. We are all learning all the time. If we are *good* therapists, we provide answers, but if we are *great* therapists, we listen to parents, we ask questions, and we do not provide all the answers! We can use A SECRET to problem-solve with parents!

So What Is the Big Secret?

The secret is: it's only a secret if you don't know it! There shouldn't be secrets! We should all strive to support the child's **quality of life, self-**

esteem (**success**), and *joie de vivre*! And we do this by making sure to clue the parents in to what we are working on—not developmentally, but in richness and in hope for gaining a real connection, an attunement, between the child and the parents.

How Did We Get Here? The Evolution of Sensory Constructs.

In 1972, Dr. A. Jean Ayres wrote, "Truth, like infinity, is to be forever approached but never reached." She encouraged us to ask and seek to answer questions. We will never have all the answers, but when we genuinely connect, use keen observation skills, focus on children's strengths, and work with parents to answer questions, we find ways to help children thrive and become their authentic selves.

While Dr. Ayres focused on sensory integration, she was a master of looking at the whole child. Relating to children was so intuitive to her and so much a part of her every interaction with the children that she didn't even seem to recognize it as a part of her treatment. Dr. Ayres thought about the components of her treatment when she wrote about it—for example, the just-right challenge, vestibular and proprioceptive input, and so on. She did not write about the quality of the therapeutic relationships because when she treated clients, it was always a part of her treatment. It was so much a part of her treatment and who she was that she assumed every OT manifested those connecting attributes. So she never wrote about it or framed it as part of her method.

OTs are trained in three areas to ensure a holistic outlook on clients: mental health, pediatrics, and physical disabilities. Therefore, all OTs have some training in pediatrics and some training in mental health, but often this training is limited. In addition to OT training, Dr. Miller sought post-graduate psychoanalytic training and participated in a three-month mentorship with Dr. Ayres. Her later formal training in DIR/Floortime (1990s) provided an opportunity to integrate psychological percepts with sensory percepts, which evolved into the STAR® frame of reference. This background informs the treatment approach at STAR Institute, the courses provided by the STAR faculty, and, of course, A SECRET.

The three authors of this book concur that while sensory information is critical, relationships and engagement are just as essential when supporting children with sensory processing challenges. That's why A SECRET is so important. It takes us beyond the lens of sensory processing and integration and opens us up to consider the child, their relationships, and their larger contexts. Our ultimate goals are *joie de vivre* (joy in life), feelings of self-*success*, self-*esteem*, and self-*regulation*, the components of a high quality of life paired with meaningful relationships.

A child who has a sensory OT is typically exposed to a series of fun and challenging but achievable activities, which should seem like play. But the play is subtly guided by the therapist in a developmental order and with specific sensory goals. Most of the OTs who come to the STAR mentorship (education) program have a good working knowledge of sensory-based principles, so they are ready to go on to the next level. The sensory knowledge a therapist brings must be accessible at a clinical (intuitive) level. That is, the language and activities of sensory processing must be a part of your underlying lexicon of knowledge. It must be available to you as implicit knowledge (Mattingly, 1991).

In the mentorship program, therapists learn to use what we call "reflection-in-action" (Schell & Schell, 2008). Experienced therapists are able to respond quickly, following a child's lead and adapting interventions in the moment to meet the child's individual sensory needs. At this level, therapists don't have to focus too much on the type of sensory information to include in the child's next activity to provide the "just-right success." Instead, the therapist quickly connects the child's preferences and actions with sensory integration theory and smoothly guides the use of equipment or play theme to meet those sensory needs. When this can be done easily and artfully, the child is able to deepen their level of engagement with the therapist and with their environment. In chapter 3, we will go into detail about why this engagement is another essential component of therapy.

What Is Just-Right Success?

Notice that we discuss **just-right success** (rather than the just-right challenge). We always focus on the competencies and strengths of our clients rather than their specific deficits. You may think 'the just-right challenge' and 'just-right success' are the same thing and that the developmental difficulty of their activities are similar. But with **just-right success**, we are focused on eliciting **JOY**! If the activity is too hard, a child may experience shame, sadness, and failure. But since we focus on the *process of interacting*, not the small developmental outcomes, it becomes easier to slowly progress in challenge level by completing activities the child experiences as successful!

What Is SPD?

As you will read in chapter 2, we are beginning to move away from the term Sensory Processing "Disorder." As research evolves, we learn more about the dynamic nature of sensory processing and integration in the brain (and body), but this work is still in progress. You will find us referring to Sensory Processing *Dimensions* (see chapter 2) and sometimes Sensory Processing *differences* or *challenges*. No matter what term we land on, the simple definition of sensory processing is taking in sensory information from the environment, organizing and interpreting it, and having an adaptive response. SPD occurs when there is a disruption in neural signals or connections somewhere between sensory receptors and higher-level brain structures. The six subtypes of SPD will be discussed in chapter 2. But before we get into the subtypes, let's look briefly at our eight sensory systems so we can understand their role in SPD.

The Eight Sensory Systems

Our eight sensory systems receive and send important information to the brain from both inside and outside our bodies. Each sensation may have a slightly different meaning to each person, depending on how an individual's brain interprets sensory input. On the basis of personal differences, such as varying interpretations of sensory information or the associations we have with sensory experiences, the brain generates a response (such as a motor or behavioral response) that is unique to the individual. So, to be able to design and implement helpful treatment activities for kids with sensory challenges, it is important to have some understanding about how sensory input either supports or challenges each child on a behavioral level.

The eight sensory systems include the five basic senses we all learned in school: sound, sight, smell, taste, and touch. In addition, two other critical sensory systems—the vestibular and proprioceptive systems—have come to be consistently included in the SPD and sensory integration literature because they are crucial to treatment. Finally, we have interoception, which includes sensation from internal organs and gives us a sense of what's going on inside our bodies.

ADDITIONAL SENSORY SYSTEMS

Sensory System	Functions & Contribution
Proprioception:	• Input from muscle and joint receptors • Provides important information about body position • Contributes to sense of self • Provides calming input, contributing to organizing the nervous system
Vestibular:	• Input from inner ear • Contributes significantly to sense of balance • Supports a foundational relationship with gravity • Provides important information about position in and movement through space • Important for sense of self

ADDITIONAL SENSORY SYSTEMS

Sensory System	Functions & Contribution
Interoception:	• Internal sensations • Awareness of basic bodily functions (thirst, hunger, temperature, need to go the bathroom) • Includes unconscious bodily functions (heart rate, respiratory rate) • Awareness of physiological responses to emotions (butterflies in our stomach, racing heart, upset stomach) • Also contributes to sense of self and self-regulation

Let's tackle each sensory system, one by one.

Auditory system: The auditory system processes and interprets information that is heard. Auditory processing includes the ability to detect the location of sound and allows us to discriminate a specific auditory target, such as a teacher's voice, from background noise, such as general noise in the classroom. It helps us distinguish sounds of safety from sounds of threat. A soothing voice can help us calm down, but a sudden yell coming from behind can send us running in the opposite direction. The auditory system is intricately tied to the vestibular system in the middle and inner ear. These systems play an important role in building self-regulation.

Visual system: The visual system involves the eyes bringing in information about the surrounding environment. It helps us distinguish subtle characteristics of a caregiver's face so we know when we are safe or when we might be in trouble. We use our visual system to read changes in facial gestures and social cues. This system, in combination with the vestibular and proprioceptive systems, is one of the ways we determine where we are in space. Together these systems allow us to make sense of the world around us, move about in response to that world, perform motor actions related to what is seen (such as catching a ball), and understand body language. Among other roles, the visual system allows us to scan a new environment to determine safety.

Olfactory system: The olfactory system is one of the first sensory systems to develop. Information from things you smell can quickly affect emotions and call up memories of emotional events. Smell is important not only for enjoying what you eat and being aware of danger (such as detecting something burning), but also for *being able* to eat. Many children have such severe sensitivities that they cannot have dinner with their families, go with their friends into stores that have a "funny" smell, or eat in restaurants.

Gustatory system: The gustatory system provides information regarding the quality or taste of foods and liquids. One of the basic roles of the gustatory system is to detect dangerous foods. Bitter foods have been shown to trigger our defense mechanisms to warn us of danger. It's no wonder children can be slow to warm up to bitter or unfamiliar foods!

Tactile system: The tactile system processes sensory information gathered from the skin. This is our largest sensory system, and it plays an important role in self-regulation. Touch is one of the earliest sensations to develop in the fetus, with studies showing responses to touch as early as 8 weeks in utero. Different types of sensory receptors in the skin receive information about touch, pressure, texture, heat, cold, and pain.

The tactile system has two divisions of touch perception. The first is the *protective system*, which makes us respond quickly to any stimulus that is perceived as potentially harmful. Often, this unexpected stimulus takes the form of light touch. For example, the protective touch system responds when a spider crawls on you or when you accidentally touch a hot stove.

The second touch subsystem is our *discriminative system*. This system gathers detailed information about characteristics of objects in our environment—things that we feel. This system tells us the difference between hard and soft, smooth and rough, hot and cold. This is the system that allows us to reach into a bag and find our keys without looking.

Vestibular system: The vestibular system defines our relationship with gravity, which is essential for developing a basic sense of safety and sense of self. It helps us understand where we are in space and plays a significant role in our sense of balance. This system provides information about head position in relation to gravity, such as the knowledge of *"I'm moving up"* or *"I'm moving down."* It also provides a sense of acceleration or deceleration (*"I'm moving faster"* and *"I'm moving slower."*) The information we receive from the vestibular system may seem abstract, but it is actually quite profound, especially in relation to self-regulation. If you've ever had vertigo, you have some idea of how dysregulating it can be to have difficulty processing vestibular information.

Proprioceptive system: The proprioceptive system allows us to feel changes in the length of our muscles and the position of our joints. The proprioceptive system sends us sensory information caused by stretching and contracting our muscles and by bending, straightening, pulling, and compressing our joints.

Our proprioceptors give us information about our body's position. For the most part, proprioception is unconscious. We don't have to look at our arms and legs to know where they are or exactly what position they are in. For example, once you've learned how to ride a bike, you don't have to watch your feet pedaling to make the bicycle wheel go around. Proprioception is known as the most grounding and organizing sensory system, so it is used often in sensory-based interventions.

Interoceptive system: Last but not least, we have interoception. What a big word for a pretty simple idea! Interoception is our sense of internal organs or bodily functions. This system provides information about how our bodies feel inside, sometimes on a conscious level, but more often on an unconscious level. For example, interoceptors tell us when we are hungry or thirsty and what's going on inside our bladder and bowels.

Summary of the 8 sensory systems: Together the tactile, vestibular, and proprioceptive systems play an essential role in sensory interventions. The combination of these three systems gives us a strong sense of self and sense of well-being. If you think about it, most of your go-to self-care or calming strategies probably involve at least one of these three systems (exercise, hugs, gentle rocking or swinging, yoga, massage, etc.)

Hopefully, you are seeing a pattern here. Our senses all play a role in creating a sense of safety, and therefore in developing an overall sense of well-being. They are all essential to the development of early relationships with our caregivers. So it should come as no surprise that we will focus much of this book on the development of regulation and relationships. You will find much more on this in chapters 3 and 8.

These are the eight sensory systems in a nutshell. The little snippets of difficulties noted previously are just that—"little peeks." They are not meant to be complete descriptions, but just enough information to help you begin to consider how disruptions in any of the sensory systems may impact a child's function. And of course, these eight sensory systems are essential to A SECRET!

What Does A SECRET Stand For?

A ttunement

S ensation
E motion Regulation
C ulture
R elationship
E nvironment
T ask

What Is A SECRET?

A SECRET (*Attunement, Sensation, Emotion Regulation, Culture, Relationship, Environment,* and *Task*) is a problem-solving tool based on the Ecological Model of Sensory Modulation (EMSM), originally created by Dr. Lucy Jane Miller and colleagues (Miller, Reisman, McIntosh, & Simon, 2001). It was first used as a clinical reasoning tool for occupational therapists and then adapted for use as a problem-solving framework for parents and teachers. Each letter represents an element which, when used in combination with each other, will help you identify ways to support your child and increase your understanding of your child's strengths and areas of challenge. This book will help you begin the problem-solving process. Our goal is for you to be able to use A SECRET to come up with unique ways to support your child in real-life situations. Rather than giving you suggestions for a sensory diet that may work for a short amount of time, A SECRET provides an opportunity to learn a sensory lifestyle.

The EMSM is a theoretical model that demonstrates the complicated and dynamic nature of Sensory Modulation Disorder (SMD) and is applicable to all SPD subtypes, including Sensory-Based Motor Disorders (SBMD) and Sensory Discrimination Disorder (SDD). The authors of the EMSM postulate that SPD can only be understood within the individual's broader life context, and A SECRET was designed to address children's needs in varied contexts or environments. Authors of the EMSM suggest that for individuals with SPD, challenges with social-emotional skills and task participation stem from an inability to respond adaptively to their environments. In other words, children with

SPD have atypical neurophysiological responses to sensory input that are reported to manifest in emotional states such as anxiety, hostility, anger, or depression; attentional difficulties, including impulsivity, hyperactivity, distractibility, or disorganization; and challenges with performing daily tasks such as dressing, self-care routines, play, and social interactions.

The components of the EMSM, both internal—*Sensation, Emotion Regulation,* and *Attention* (now *Attunement*)—and external—*Culture, Environment, Relationship,* and *Task*—interact in a dynamic fashion to challenge or support an individual. A SECRET is a clinical reasoning framework for these internal and external dimensions that allows a clinician to find a just-right balance between supports and demands, thereby supporting children in successfully participating in daily life activities, and more importantly, to improve their quality of life.

A SECRET has been further developed as a problem-solving tool for caregivers. This tool provides parents with a deeper understanding of their children (Gee & Peterson, 2016), including their strengths, challenges, and sensory and social-emotional needs. It is our hope that A SECRET will also increase parents'/teachers'/caregivers' understanding of the need for self-care and self-reflection as essential factors in caring for their children and the family system.

How Will A SECRET Help Me Support My Child?

We use *A SECRET* to identify your child's strengths and find their joy and success. Using those strengths, we can respond positively when challenges occur in therapy, in your home, and in the community. We examine the factors contributing to an observed challenge and modify or use the other components of *A SECRET* to support the challenge area. The goal of OT for children is to develop automatic and successful responses to sensation so that daily occupations or skills can be performed, self-esteem can grow, self-regulation can develop, and social participation can be fostered. These foundational abilities support specific family goals.

How Do I Use the Components of A SECRET to Problem-Solve?

Each element of A SECRET will help you identify ways to support your child and increase your understanding of your child's strengths and areas of challenge. This book will help you begin the problem-solving process, but our goal is for you to be able to use this tool to come up with unique ways to support your child in *real-life* situations.

Within each category of A SECRET, you can identify ways to support your child by asking the following questions:

Attunement (to child and self):
- When does my child shine and engage the most?
- What sensory differences do I recognize in my child?
- What observations can I make about my child's ability to self-regulate?
- How does my stress level impact my child?
- How does my arousal or stress level change when my child is melting down?

- What do I need to do to regulate my own arousal so I can co-regulate my child?
- Is my child aware of changes in their arousal or emotional state?

Sensation:
- Which sensations help my child feel the most organize or calm?
- How can I use sensory tools to support my child's attention and engagement?
- Which sensory systems are a challenge for my child?
- How does my child respond to the intensity of sensations?
- How does my child respond to expected sensations?

Emotion Regulation:
- When does my child show the most control over emotions?
- How does my child respond to *big* emotions?
- What tools can I use to help my child regulate emotions?
- What tools can I use to increase my child's awareness of emotions?

Culture:
- Is my child more regulated and engaged with predictable routines?
- What routines does my family have for self-care?
- What part of my family's culture (habits and routines) can be changed to support regulation?

Relationship:
- Which relationships are most supportive for my child?
- Who are the *safe* people in my child's life?

- Is there something in the relationships experienced by my child that is causing their responses?
- Does my child need closer support or more space?

Environment:

- What in the environment is optimal for my child?
- How can those environmental factors be modified?

Task:

- What tasks does my child enjoy?
- Which games or activities make my child the most calm?
- Does my child prefer clear expectations?
- Should I change my expectations when my child is dysregulated?
- How can the task be modified so my child can be successful?

What's Different about This Edition?

If you know the first edition of this book, you will quickly see that this edition is very different. Instead of organizing the chapters according to SPD subtype, we've focused on the elements of A SECRET. This is a very deliberate change for two reasons. First, SPD is not so black and white that we can consider interventions and strategies based on specific subtypes. It is most common that children have combinations of challenges across sensory systems and subtypes. Rather than classifying strategies according to subtype, it is more helpful to understand each element of A SECRET in detail, and then consider how it applies to your child and family. Second, each element of A SECRET plays an essential role in creating a sensory lifestyle. Examining each element in this way provides more opportunity for considering how to fit strategies into your family (or classroom) culture.

Another big change is the shift from A = *Attention* to A = *Attunement*. Over the years, we have come to realize that *Attunement* is one of the most important tools in our toolbelts. As therapists/parents/teachers/caregivers, we must attune to (be aware of or attentive to) our children and their sensory differences, and to ourselves! We need to pay attention to changes in arousal regulation in our children and in ourselves. Chapter 5 goes into detail about *Attunement*, so we won't discuss it here, but we do want to point out that this is an important change from the first edition.

You will see that we are also emphasizing the interactions between the elements of A SECRET. Many of the strategies that we suggest in one element of A SECRET will also fit into other elements. For instance, modeling awareness of your own emotions (*Emotion Regulation*) may also support your *Relationship* with your child. Creating a *Culture* of consistent morning routines with simple heavy work activities (*Sensation*) may improve transitions. We use this symbol throughout the book to indicate these interactions between elements of A SECRET.

Figure 1.1

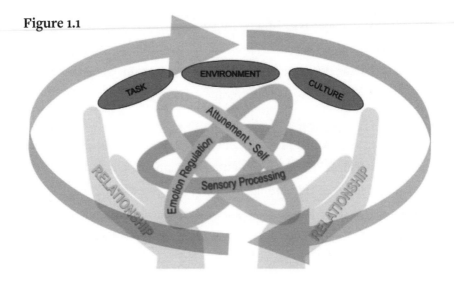

Figure 1.1 This image depicts the internal (*Attunement, Sensation, Emotion Regulation*) and external (*Task, Environment, Culture*) elements of A SECRET. The hands represent *Relationship* as an essential element that supports and holds the framework together. This image further indicates the dynamic, interpersonal nature of A SECRET, demonstrating that within relationships, we use all elements to foster the development of the whole person.

Finally, in this edition we have added reflections and examples of A SECRET for each element. We encourage you to use the reflections to problem-solve what we call *process points* for each element. We define *process points* as **guiding principles for individualized and dynamic recommendations to support sensory processing and regulation in varied contexts**. They are really the *WHY* behind dynamic OT strategies and recommendations. You can also think about *process points* as supportive concepts that help with a therapist's clinical reasoning during OT sessions and that ultimately translate into empowering parental problem-solving at home.

How to Use This Book

Each element of A SECRET is essential to supporting individuals with SPD. The beauty of this problem-solving framework is that it gives a big-picture view of how to support your child in different contexts. We've highlighted the importance of *Attunement* and *Relationship* in this edition. We all wish there were a quick fix or a magic bullet to build self-regulation and support success in our kids with SPD, but the truth is it's not as simple as a sensory diet. External factors (*Culture, Environment, Task*) are changing every moment, and our responses to those factors are influencing our internal responses (*Sensation, Emotion Regulation*). *Attunement* and *Relationship* are the real magic. These elements provide the glue for pulling A SECRET together and for helping our children thrive.

References

Miller, L. J., Reisman, J., McIntosh, D. N., & Simon, J. (2001). The ecological model of sensory modulation: Performance of children with fragile X syndrome, autism, ADHD, and SMD. *Sensory integration and developmental disabilities*. Therapy Skill Builders.

Schell, B. B., & Schell, J. W. (2008). Professional reasoning as the basis of practice. *Clinical and professional reasoning in occupational therapy*, 3-12.

Example

A SECRET for problem-solving: The following suggestions are recommended to support continued development of self-regulation and social-emotional skills.

A SECRET

Challenge Area	Attunement	Sensation	Emotion Regulation

• Self-regulation
 	
• Spitting and other aggressive behaviors at school
	• Closely observe patterns in Sam's moments of dysregulation
	
	• Proximity— get down on his eye level
	
	• Attune to your own arousal changes— create a plan for regulating yourself when Sam is melting down
		• Supportive sensory input for Sam:
		  * Deep pressure
		  * Soft tactile input (blanket)
		
		• Sam's arousal tends to increase with the following input:
		  * Movement
		  * Auditory
		  * Tactile input
		  * Light or unexpected
			• Set clear limits
			
			1. Listen or attune to Sam's sensory or regulation needs
			
			2. Set firm & kind limit in advance (no spitting)
			
			3. Be present & allow upset feelings (see handout)

Example (continued)

STRENGTHS: Sam is playful, creative, and kind. He enjoys reading, playing with his little brother, and making friends. Sam is learning self-regulation skills. He benefits from support (co-regulation) from caregivers when he is in a new or stressful environment.

A SECRET *(CONTINUED)*

Culture	Relationship	Environment	Task

• Be consistent with firm & kind limits
 	
• Set aside a regular time for one-on-one play with Sam (follow his lead in play)
	• Sam has strong relationships with his parents and responds well to co-regulation
	
	• Identify safe person at school who can help with co-regulation and slow down plan
	
	• Feelings are easier to work through when Sam has a safe and attentive listener
		* Sam demonstrates improved regulation in small, quiet environments
		
		* Locate a safe space where Sam can slow down when his arousal is high
			• Set plan in advance with Sam:
			  * Set limit
			  * Identify safe space
			  * Choose safe person
			  * Have Sam assist with choosing calming sensory tools
			
			• Help Sam understand that this is NOT a timeout or a punishment. This is to help his body calm down

CHAPTER 2

SPD PAST, PRESENT, AND FUTURE:

A DIMENSIONAL APPROACH TO EVALUATING INDIVIDUAL DIFFERENCES IN SENSORY PROCESSING

The purpose of this chapter is to provide a brief background of SPD—past, present, and future. In this chapter, we offer an overview of the progression of SPD in the past decade and discuss where the science is headed. In the rest of the book, we will continue to use the nosology, or classification system, that was identified in 2007 by Dr. Miller and colleagues. Here, we will provide a new view of sensory processing from a dimensional perspective. We believe it's helpful to recognize (in a very simplified way) how sensory information is processed and integrated in the brain. When we view sensory processing and integration from this perspective, we can more easily understand the needs of our children, problem-solve ways to support them, and perhaps shift our expectations and begin to understand our children better.

Why Is SPD a Controversial Diagnosis?

SPD is a controversial diagnosis for a number of reasons. First, there is no standardized norm–referenced assessment of SPD ... at least not yet. Since 2002, Dr. Miller and colleagues have been working on a new test to identify SPD, and there are other assessments in the works, but currently there is not a published test to assess SPD. Healthcare professionals, usually occupational therapists, identify SPD based on a combination of clinical observations and parental report.

Second, diagnosing SPD is quite complex. There are eight sensory systems that must be considered when identifying SPD, which include the five basic sensory systems: tactile (touch), visual (sight), auditory (hearing), gustatory (taste), and olfactory (smell). There are also three additional, less familiar senses: proprioception, vestibular, and interoception. Proprioception and vestibular (as you will see throughout this book) are essential to OT intervention for SPD, and, of course, to A SECRET.

Third, SPD is a relatively new "diagnosis" (remember, it isn't an official diagnosis) with a wide range of symptoms, or what we call individual differences. SPD is usually identified by OTs with post-professional training in the assessment and treatment of sensory processing and integration challenges. But there is still some disagreement among healthcare professionals (even among OTs) as to the classification of SPD and the observable behaviors related to the disorder.

SPD Nosology: Past, Present and Future

What is a Nosology?

Nosology refers to the branch of medical science dealing with the classification of diseases. In order to confirm a diagnosis, it is necessary to understand the causes, symptoms, and effects that a disease has on function. A nosology organizes these factors to assist with identification of a disorder, but more importantly, to aid in research. In order to perform rigorous research studies, it is necessary to start with a clear means of identifying your population of interest. This was one of the main reasons for the proposed nosology that we currently use for SPD. With a nosology, we can study a homogeneous or similar group of subjects to better understand the disorder as a whole.

SPD Defined and the Current Nosology

The current classification scheme was first suggested by Miller, Anzaone, Lane, Cermak, and Osten (2007). This nosology was based on an educated guess from existing data of patterns or subtypes of SPD. The patterns were expected to shift over the years as more scientific evidence became available. In fact, in the absence of hard, objective data, such as genetic evidence, a continuously shifting model makes sense, as new data are published to support or refute the existing model. It was expected that we would begin with this nosology and come closer to the actual subtypes over time. The investigators believed it was possible that SPD would ultimately not be identified as a distinct disorder, but as two or three separate disorders or as a spectrum of dysfunction across many diagnoses.

As clinicians, this situation can be distressing. We want to "know" what the subtypes are and may not want the patterns to keep evolving and changing. But for a researcher, change is important and positive. It suggests that you have additional clarifying data that bring you closer to the "truth." We use quotes because in the field of neurodevelopmental and behavioral disorders, "truth" is only approached but not reached— at least not until a more objective method of diagnosis is developed by the scientific community.

SPD Defined

Each of us has unique neurological wiring. Some of us process input with more efficiency, and others with less efficiency. This accounts in part for our "individual differences"—what makes us distinct from each other. What makes us functional is whether or not we can make sense of the information in our environment and respond to both internal signals and external demands with meaningful and purposeful actions. "Typically developing" or "neurotypical" children have differently wired systems that may make it easier for them to move fluidly through environmental challenges. They may make friends more easily, engage well at school, and transition easily from one setting to the next.

Critical to the successful negotiation of one's life path is the ability to process sensory information. Sensory processing requires a complex set of brain functions, including detecting, modulating, integrating, and accurately interpreting information received through the sensory systems. Processing sensory input enables meaningful responses in motor, language, cognitive, behavioral, and other related domains. Sensations inform people about the characteristics of their internal states and the qualities of their external surroundings. Recent research suggests three primary classifications of SPD and six separate subtypes.

What defines a subtype of SPD is a controversial subject in the field. That's because no one has enough data to really answer the question of exactly *what the SPD subtypes are*, so most models are theoretical in nature. When the empirical data are lacking, people argue on the basis of belief systems rather than knowledge.

So what does this mean for parents? Parents need to have evaluations conducted by clinicians who have been well-trained in SPD and have studied with and been mentored by experienced, high-level experts in the field. For parents and children, what matters are the strengths and challenges of the individual child. We believe that the more elements of SPD that can be tested and observed individually, the better understanding a clinician will have of any particular child. If these elements can be addressed separately, then the child can be supported within the context of their family. Thus, we propose using the current nosology to evaluate all the elements that might be affecting a child. Then, all the pieces of knowledge gained can be put back together to paint a picture of the whole child.

Subtypes of SPD

SPD occurs on a spectrum, from mildly affected individuals coping with their sensory challenges to more severely affected individuals who have great difficulties with performing routine daily tasks. The latter group may have difficulty functioning scholastically, vocationally, recreationally, and socially. These children may have motor challenges and quite often exhibit pronounced anxiety, withdrawal, depression, behavioral problems, alcohol and/or substance abuse (depending on their age), or combinations of these problems.

SPD has been shown in research to affect 5% to 16% of children. The causes of SPD have not yet been identified in definitive research, but a few studies implicate genetic factors (Goldsmith et al., 2006), birth complications (May-Benson, Koomar, & Teasdale, 2009), and environmental factors (Schneider, Moore, & Gajewski, 2008) as potential causes.

Figure 2.1

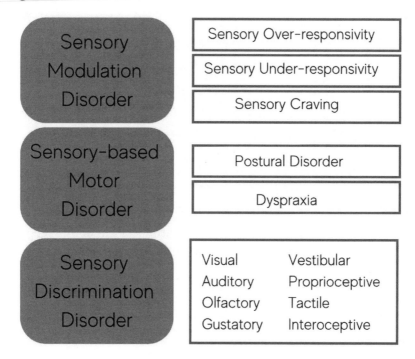

Figure 2.1. This chart provides a visual summary of the six basic sub-types of SPD using the current nosology. Note: Thank you to Dr Sarah A. Schoen for her assistance in editing these definitions.

An overview of each subtype follows. Along the way, you will "meet" children who demonstrate salient behaviors and characteristics specific to each one.

Sensory Modulation Disorder

Sensory modulation disorder has three subtypes: sensory over-responsivity, sensory under-responsivity, and sensory craving.

Sensory over-responsivity: Toby is a child with sensory over-responsivity. He appears quite skeptical and anxious of others, especially strangers. You may feel as if there is a barrier of barbed wire around Toby, and it's hard to get close to him. It feels like Toby is protecting himself from everyone and everything. It takes time to get to know Toby, but once his guard comes down, Toby is a kind, caring, and engaged child. The process of getting to know Toby is like unpeeling an artichoke to get at the meaty insides.

Children with sensory over-responsivity are very reactive to small amounts of stimuli. They often experience a sense of overload in one or multiple sensory systems. Sensory information for children like Toby may be experienced as painful and scary, triggering a flight-or-fight reaction during which the child wants to run away and hide.

Sensory under-responsivity: Sergio is having a snack with his classmates in Ms. Garcia's classroom. The room is noisy, with kids laughing and talking. Sergio, a first-grade student, is having pudding for a snack. He has sensory under-responsivity, indicated by his dreamy, lethargic-looking state and his tendency to "melt" into the ground or into his seat. What's most intriguing is that despite all the noise around the class, Sergio seems impervious to it. You call to him, "Sergio," but there's no response. You try again, a little louder this time, but still no response. This time you try coming closer, and with a little shoulder tap and louder voice, you repeat, "Sergio!" "Oh hi," Sergio says, noticing you in the classroom for the first time. You ask, "Do you want to play a game?" Sergio responds with a blank stare, and then shakes his head after a pause. "No!"

Children with sensory under-responsivity process sensory information slowly, requiring increased frequency and/or intensity before they notice sensory input. Children like Sergio appear to have a poor inner drive and a lack of initial desire to explore and play.

Sensory craving: Rebecca is an overzealous, little kindergartener. She rushes over to greet you and says, "I like your red hair and your shiny necklace! Hey, what's all that stuff you're carrying around?" She moves closer to you with no awareness of personal boundaries and is now practically sitting on your lap, anxious to see your new toys and games. She starts to pull some of the toys out of your arms.

"Wait one minute," you say to her. Rebecca moves quickly, and her actions are somewhat unpredictable.

You say, "Hey Rebecca, what did one penny say to the other?" "I don't know, what?" answers Rebecca.

"Let's get together and make some sense!"

She smiles and retorts, "Do you know where a snowman keeps his money?" "No," you reply, "Where?"

"In a snow bank!" she says, laughing.

Rebecca has a great sense of humor that makes you both smile. You connect emotionally for a brief moment, each of you acknowledging that you are having fun and kidding around. Okay, so for the moment you have Rebecca's undivided attention. You turn around to get something from your bag that you brought for Rebecca to play with, and when you turn back to her, she is gone. The five seconds you spent digging around in your bag was too long for her to wait—she lost interest and is now off doing something else in another location.

A prevalent belief in the field is that sensory craving (or sensory seeking, as it is commonly called) is caused by children not getting enough stimulation. Those who believe this generally think that sensory cravers, like sensory under-responders, need strong intensity and frequent and large amounts of stimulation to "fill them up." We have found this to be somewhat of a myth. We have data to suggest that children who crave sensation, like Rebecca, are in their own modulation category. Unlike children with sensory over- and under-responsivity, sensory cravers become more disorganized with sensory input unless it's provided in a very specific manner, with a functional goal, and for a specific parameter of time. Cravers can't get enough sensation! They will try to get all the spinning, bouncing, jumping, touching, or singing that they can get, but it's never enough. When these children get more input, they begin to spiral out of control and dysregulate.

Sensory *craving* is also different than sensory *seeking*. Children with any combination of SPD subtypes will *seek* sensory input. The difference between *seeking* and *craving* is that a child who is *seeking* sensory input is looking for that input to organize their nervous system. They usually won't be doing this on a conscious level and may need our help to begin recognizing strategies to stay regulated. In the case of a sensory seeker, the child is often looking for the most organizing types of sensation (proprioception, vestibular, tactile). As usual, this is individual. We all seek the input that is most organizing for us. We can't expect that any one type of sensation will work for every child.

Sensory-Based Motor Disorder

Two subtypes of SPD fall under this category—postural disorder and dyspraxia.

Postural disorder: It is circle time in Ms. Tello's room, and Elena and her classmates are all sitting on the carpet. Elena stands out among her peers, with her body slumped over so close to the floor that her little trunk is in a "C" shape. Elena seems genuinely uncomfortable while trying to sit up. She looks even more uncomfortable when she attempts to move. The class stands, and Elena's knees buckle beneath her. Her peers take a break and are going outside to the playground. Elena reaches out to grab your hand for assistance in getting up. "Can we play here instead? I don't really like going on the playground. I'm not a good climber. I hate the swings," she says, winded and speaking in short sentences.

Children with postural disorder have difficulty processing sensory stimulation from the proprioceptive (information from the joints and muscles of the body) and vestibular (sense of movement in relation to the pull of gravity) systems. Like Elena, they feel uncomfortable with body-position changes. They have weak muscle tone and difficulty sustaining static positions, and they may appear loose or "floppy" when moving.

Dyspraxia: Arturo is tripping over his own untied shoelaces and falling down on the floor. The teacher begins a morning exercise routine, and Arturo stands back, watching the other kids do the routine. This routine was taught by his teacher yesterday, and the class has quickly caught on, except Arturo.

"Arturo, can you show me how these steps are done so I can do the exercises too?" you ask.

Arturo answers, "Just watch; you will see how my friends do it."

"Okay," you think. "He might know what needs to be done, but he just can't seem to organize the steps to do it."

Arturo and other children with dyspraxia have difficulty making a plan for action. They often prefer to watch others, because they are challenged by unfamiliar movements with multiple steps, like the new exercises shown to the class. They may avoid unfamiliar environments or activities, have difficulty with group play, and often joke around when a task is too difficult. Children with dyspraxia may also have difficulty with higher-level planning tasks such as getting homework from the dining room table, to their backpacks, and turned into the teacher. They may struggle with organizing their time to complete a large project or even getting out the door in the morning. Transitions, especially to an unfamiliar place, may be very taxing for these children (and their parents).

Sensory discrimination disorder: You watch Ramira color a flat sheet of paper that is then supposed to be cut with scissors and taped together to make a box (Figure 2.2). Ramira is using so much force that the crayons keep breaking, and she is making holes in the sheet. She grasps the scissors upside-down to make cuts, and her cutting strokes are small and way outside the lines. When she tries to tape the sides of the box together, she has trouble manipulating the tape, and it gets all tangled up in her fingers. Ramira clearly has no idea which sides of the box are taped to each other. She is becoming extremely frustrated.

Figure 2.2

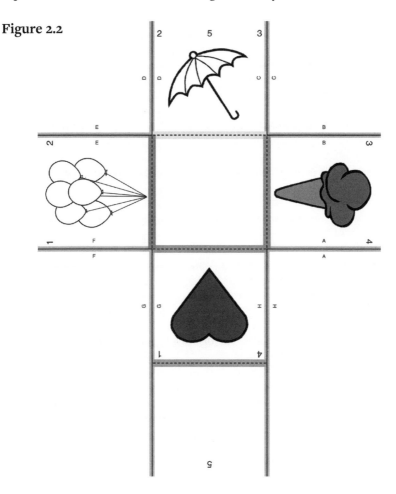

Figure 2.2. Paper box task (a testing item) from the Goal-Oriented Assessment of Life Skills Test, Research Edition, by Miller, Oakland, and Herzberg (Western Psychological Services, 2011).

"Hi, Ramira. Your teacher asked me to come see you today to find out if I could help you with projects like this."

In a loud voice, Ramira responds, "I don't need help! I'm done now anyway."

Ramira stands and pushes her chair under the table. The desk moves two feet forward because she uses so much force. Ramira seems unaware that the desk moved unnecessarily.

Sensory discrimination disorder is the third major pattern of SPD. Children with this subtype have difficulties interpreting and distinguishing messages within one or more sensory systems, which can result in confusion, frustration, and often very slow work. In the preceding vignette, Ramira demonstrated discriminatory challenges with the following systems: visual (difficulty seeing where to cut), proprioceptive (coloring through the paper), and auditory (using a voice level inappropriate for the setting).

As mentioned at the beginning of this chapter, the above SPD subtype terminology will be used throughout this book. However, we want to briefly take a look at the future of SPD.

Do We Need a New Nosology?

Adaptations to terminology have been suggested over the years, including changing the term sensory integration dysfunction (SID) to sensory processing disorder (SPD). However, we would like to look at the wide range of empirical data expected over the next few years before proposing another new nosology or a change in terminology. Naming SPD and categorizing the symptoms have been useful in validating parents' concerns. They have had a strong effect on specifying sensory differences in autism in the 5th edition of the Diagnostic and Statistical Manual (DSM). They have also helped set the stage by establishing groundwork to identify subtypes of SPD for additional studies.

Where Are We Going?

The National Institute of Mental Health (NIMH) recently called for a new system as a way "to transform diagnosis by incorporating genetics, imaging, cognitive science, and other levels of information to lay the foundation for a new classification system." This system, called Research Domain Criteria (RDoC), was revised in 2019 to include both sensory and motor functioning (Harrison and Aziz-Zadek, 2019). The purpose of the RDoC is to study all criteria across a dimension of function (from function to dysfunction). Criteria will be examined from as many frameworks as possible, from very small (cellular level) to very complex (functional level). Some terminology is neurological (e.g., signal detection, detection of a stimulus, lack of response to a stimulus) while other aspects are described behaviorally (e.g., registration, over-responsivity, sensory attenuation, habituation). In fact, many of these behaviors can be attributed to poor regulation (also called modulation) of responses. The goal of the RDoC is to relate the two levels to one another.

Obviously, more knowledge and understanding of SPD will come with future research. We feel comfortable knowing that in the next quarter century, this research will question brain networks, neurochemistry, and neural firing to explain the facets of disrupted sensory processing on these three levels of brain function:

HYPOTHESIZED NEURAL UNDERPINNINGS OF SPD LEVELS OF BRAIN FUNCTION

General Brain Level	Anatomical Considerations	Functions
High-level functioning	Cortex and other association areas, other high-level structures such as most of the frontal lobe	*Evaluate and respond:* Discriminate, plan, and respond after evaluating sensory input
Mid-level processing	Cerebellum, limbic system and others; systems lower than the cortex but not as low as subcortical structures	*Assimilate:* Integrate, process, and relay sensory data
Low-level abilities	Subcortical structures and autonomic nervous system	*Regulate:* Perceive, protect, and immediately react

Good Reasons to Wait for a New Nosology

Perhaps it is provident that a new nosology has not been drafted yet. A controversy exists about whether SPD and many other conditions are "disorders" or "dimensions" of behavior. The word *disorder* is defined as the diagnostic boundary outside of which a person may be labeled "atypical or disordered." The cut point of "normal" is often based on arbitrary divisions between normal and abnormal to simplify the categorization for clinical and research purposes. Even though most professionals believe many psychological and physiological behaviors exist along a continuum, the DSM sets thresholds to differentiate normal versus disordered using a categorical system—categories within which behavior is considered abnormal. This creates high rates of comorbidity (overlapping diagnoses), because the symptoms across disorders are extremely heterogeneous (broad). An individual's condition will therefore often include multiple diagnoses.

Moving away from this narrow, categorial view of disorders, Sensory Processing Dimensions (SPD) are believed by many scientists to exist on a continuum. With this focus on sensory processing as a dimension, we are less concerned with the identification of a disorder. This is because we are seeing sensory processing "dimensions" impacting function across a wide range of diagnoses (comorbidities). But we are not only looking at physical or mental health diagnoses; we are recognizing that sensory processing dimensions affect all of us and contribute to our well-being and resiliency. Rather than focusing on a diagnosis, we are now seeing sensory health and wellness as our overarching outcome. You don't need to have a "disorder" to benefit from attention to your individual sensory differences. You don't have to have a disorder to benefit from A SECRET!

So maybe it's good we do not have a widely accepted diagnosis yet! Well, it's good for the science, but not for the clients, who eagerly await insurance benefits and services. Thus, we continue to strive to understand SPD and SPD interventions. We support and develop research, mentor advanced clinicians, and work with parents to improve understanding of our children. We have developed and enhanced A SECRET to build self-regulation capacities, strengthen parent-child-relationships, promote self-esteem, and foster joie de vivre.

Maria's Story

Maria is a 3-year-old girl from Romania who was adopted after spending more than two years in an orphanage with minimal environmental stimulation and emotional interaction. In Romania, she slept in a small crib in a dimly lit room with 20 other babies. She was rarely allowed to crawl or move anywhere except inside her tiny crib. When she was fed, her bottle was propped against a blanket, and she was rarely held or cuddled. When she was old enough to hold the bottle herself, her caretakers stopped paying attention at a basic level.

Melinda and Denzel Walton had been looking forward to this adoption for over a year, dreaming about the beautiful baby girl they knew only from a photograph. They despaired when they finally went to Romania to pick Maria up a few months after her second birthday. She alternated constantly between fits of screaming and staring blankly into space.

When we saw Maria at the STAR Center, she had turned 3 years old and had been with the Walton family for several months. Table 2.4 summarizes her sensory modulation by each sensory system observed during her occupational therapy evaluation.

Table 2.4 Maria's Profile.

CHALLENGES IN SENSORY PROCESSING DIMENSIONS			
Challenges in Sensory Modulation Dimensions			
SPD Subtypes:	SOR*	SUR*	SC*
Visual	✓		
Auditory		✓	
Olfactory (smell)		✓	
Gustatory (taste)		✓	
Tactile (touch)	✓		
Vestibular (relation to gravity)			✓
Proprioception (position & pressure of muscles/joints)			✓
Interoception (sensations from organs)		✓	

SENSORY SYSTEMS

* SOR: Sensory over-responsivity   SUR: Sensory under-responsivity   SC: Sensory craving

CHALLENGES IN SENSORY PROCESSING DIMENSIONS *(continued)*			
Challenges in Sensory-Based Motor Dimensions			
SPD Subtypes:	SOR	SUR	SC
Postural Challenges			
Dyspraxia			
Challenges in Sensory Discrimination Dimensions			
Tactile			
Vestibular			
Auditory			

SENSORY SYSTEMS

Maria's evaluation revealed challenges in all sensory processing dimensions. Given her history and severe over-responsivities, it was not a surprise to see higher-level challenges with motor-based and discrimination dimensions. The severity of Maria's auditory, tactile, and visual over-responsivities greatly impacted her regulation and her ability to connect with her parents. Naturally, she was sensitive to touch (also called tactile defensiveness) because she had hardly been touched, other than when her diaper needed changing or when she was being poked and prodded during checkups and vaccinations. This led to a resistance to being held. She was not able to benefit from typical co-regulation or calming strategies. While all areas of sensory processing would eventually be addressed, the therapist began intervention with a focus on regulation, which included sensory modulation. Of course, a crucial piece of this intervention process included supporting and developing Maria's relationship with her parents.

Maria's therapist worked with the Waltons to help them recognize Maria's sensory differences. She pointed out Maria's sensory preferences and sensory challenges. As they began to understand how Maria responded to sensory information in her environment, the Waltons were able to create a safe and welcoming space for Maria. This space not only included the home environment, but also their interactions with Maria. They learned how to adjust their expectations and their affect level (intensity of facial gestures, volume and tone of voice, body language). Within weeks they were feeling connected and able to playfully interact with Maria for 15-20 minutes at a time.

Not long into Maria's therapy, she learned to walk and even run for short spurts. Her parents were thrilled. They had been told she might not ever walk. But now that she was upright, all she seemed to do was walk-run at full speed. She'd keep moving quickly, even if it meant crashing into people or furniture. When she crashed, she turned and ran in the opposite direction. Maria's sensory modulation and regulation challenges were improving, and now her sensory-based motor challenges were becoming apparent. She was unable to stand still or control her body while she was moving through her environment. Her sensory discrimination challenges also played a role in her motor development. Her therapist continued to use a relationship-based approach to make Maria feel safe (and to deepen her relationship with her parents) but slightly shifted the goal of her intervention to include motor-based and discrimination outcomes.

What's critical to understand is that accurate identification drives treatment planning. As therapists, we need to constantly ask questions and seek answers. Our evaluation is never over. We are always problem-solving to better understand and support our children and families. In the following chapters, we will briefly discuss assessment and intervention for children with SPD, with detailed information on each element of A SECRET. We hope this information will help parents ask and answer their own questions, problem-solve strategies for their families, and feel more confident in collaborating with their child's therapist.

References

Goldsmith, H. H., Van Hulle, C. A., Arneson, C. L., Schreiber, J. E., & Gernsbacher, M. A. (2006). A population-based twin study of parentally reported tactile and auditory defensiveness in young children. *Journal of Abnormal Child Psychology, 34*(3), 378-392.

Harrison, L. A., Kats, A., Williams, M. E., & Aziz-Zadeh, L. (2019). The importance of sensory processing in mental health: a proposed addition to the Research Domain Criteria (RDoC) and suggestions for RDoC 2.0. *Frontiers in Psychology, 10*, 103.

Miller, L. J., Anzalone, M. E., Lane, S. J., Cermak, S. A., & Osten, E. T. (2007). Concept evolution in sensory integration: a proposed nosology for diagnosis. *American Journal of Occupational Therapy, 61*(2), 135-140.

CHAPTER 3

UNDERPINNINGS OF
A SECRET

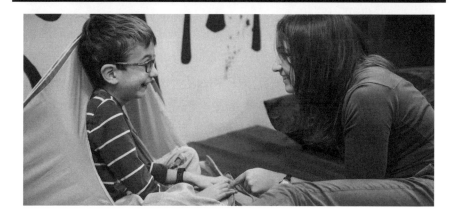

Introduction

We like to say that A SECRET is occupational therapy (OT) at its best!
Like many other models, A SECRET uses a dynamic systems view
(Thelen, 2005), which includes considering each child or individual
(we use the word "individual" to refer to the adolescents and adults we
treat) within their own unique contexts, such as their family and community systems. When we evaluate a child, we start with the caregivers'
input, because what parents, teachers, and other caregivers observe is
essential! Of course, we do a thorough assessment, including clinical
observations, but we want to consider more than the child alone. We
are not in all contexts with a child, so parent and teacher reports are

crucial. This broad view helps us understand that development is not a linear process, especially for our sensory kids. SPD affects the whole child and the whole family. That is why we use A SECRET to explore the dynamic roles of the environment, relationships, and neurobiology, then consider how these pieces come together when we create an individualized support plan.

Human development is a complex and dynamic process that spans a lifetime. This process is especially complicated for individuals with sensory challenges, and A SECRET was created to meet that complexity, packaged in a form that makes it as concrete or elaborate as necessary. For those of you familiar with Dr. Lucy Jane Miller and her work, it should be no surprise that A SECRET is grounded in research and evidence-based practice. Remember that evidence-based practice doesn't only include research. The therapist's clinical experience is an essential piece of the puzzle, but not the most important one. The most important one is the experience and perspective of the family! A SECRET is made to combine all of these pieces. The therapist should come with a basic knowledge of relevant research, their own professional experience, and the ability to listen and ask questions of the individual or family, or of the teacher for those working in schools. Our team isn't complete without the family!

This chapter provides a brief overview of the science behind A SECRET and a glimpse into the complexity of the work we do. Our goal is not to provide an exhaustive review of the research behind SPD or to provide an in-depth understanding of the neurological foundations of SPD, but we offer the basics in this chapter. We hope this chapter will help parents, teachers, and other caregivers understand why we work the way we do and why we prioritize play. Our goal is to help you understand our perspective related to the behaviors you are seeing at home and at school, and to help you connect with your child even more deeply.

Scientific Foundations of A SECRET

The idea of the acronym A SECRET began with a study in 2001 exploring internal factors (*Attention, Sensation,* and *Emotion*) and external factors (*Culture, Relationship, Environment,* and *Task*) affecting children with Sensory Modulation Disorder (SMD). In this study, Dr. Miller and her colleagues highlighted the complex and dynamic nature of SMD and laid the groundwork for the idea that SPD can only be understood within a child's broader life context. It is not enough to consider sensory strategies alone; we must learn to look at the whole picture. We have to pay attention to the environment, context, and relationships, and how they all interact. Using a single strategy or activity, or a static *sensory diet*, doesn't work for our complex sensory kids. Sensory diets may be helpful, but they only work in a specific situation. A sensory strategy that works on a good day in the "just-right" situation will not work when a child is stressed or when their arousal is heightened. For that matter, it won't work when the parent or caregiver is stressed (and this is why A SECRET always includes care for the caregiver)!

Current research supports this idea that the easy answer, the magic bullet that we all want, simply isn't there. Thanks to brain imaging research, we now know that we are not looking to change one part of the brain at a time. People with SPD or any sensory challenge have differences in the whole brain, specifically the connections between different parts of the brain (Chang et al., 2014; Owen et al., 2013). Then, of course, we know that these connections are not just in the brain, but throughout the entire body. The STAR frame of reference© uses a sensory- and relationship-based approach that is constructed around the latest research, the extensive experiences of master clinicians, and parents' perspectives. Grounded in Dr. Miller's years of experience and the supporting work of many other disciplines, researchers, and clinicians, A SECRET is a framework that organizes our knowledge and our ability to look at each person with a new lens, a curiosity to ask and answer questions.

When we consider both internal and external factors that affect a child's arousal and behavior, we learn to attune or pay full attention to the child, and we may shift our perspective of their behavior. This means we start by recognizing a child's strengths, understand the stress caused by learning a new task, identify environmental stressors, and learn to anticipate challenges in advance. Perhaps most importantly, we can see the benefits (true neurological and developmental benefits) of play. We begin to use playful interactions (**R**–*relationship* and **E**–*emotion regulation*) to support a child's arousal regulation and, in turn, their success with daily tasks and organized behavior.

Being the dynamic tool that it is, A SECRET is ever-changing and adaptable. This means that new evidence and theories, new science, is incorporated into creating the best possible problem-solving tool for children and families living with SPD. For those of you interested in the science behind A SECRET, this chapter is for you! This obviously isn't the forum for in-depth scientific writing, but we will give you an overview of the science and reasoning behind the tool we call A SECRET, which also provides insight into all we consider when we are working with kids and families. It may even help you understand why therapy at STAR Institute does just look *like* play!

Strategies in the *relationship* and *emotion regulation* elements of A SECRET are connected to Dr. Miller's background in psychotherapy (along with OT) and relationship-based therapy. They are strongly based on the work of Dr. Stanley Greenspan and Dr. Serena Weider, the Developmental Individual Difference Relationship-Based Therapy (DIR®). DIR® is an intervention model used by OTs, mental health practitioners, and other healthcare providers, and it can be used by parents in the home. Because it is so individualized and is highly related to individualized processing, this approach is difficult to study, yet research is showing improvements in parent-child interactions and social-emotional development, and decreased parent stress when parents are coached in using this technique at home (Pajareya & Nopmaneejumruslers, 2012; Solomon et al., 2012). Many of the strategies often used in the elements *relationship*, *emotion regulation*, and even *culture* are elements of A SECRET which stem from the DIR approach.

The Science behind Play and Relationships

Play is the occupation of children, and it is important to all of us for a balanced life. The field of Interpersonal Neurobiology (IPNB), developed by Dr. Daniel Siegel (2012) and Dr. Allan Schore, provides the *why* behind using a play- and relationship-based approach to intervention.

In this section, we reference *The Interpersonal Neurobiology of Play* by Theresa Kestly (2014), which specifically explains the neurological benefits of play. Dr. Kestly's work helps us understand why we include the *Emotion Regulation* and *Relationship* elements in A SECRET, in addition to the ever-important *Sensory* element. As occupational therapists, we believe play is a child's most important occupation. This makes sense when you know how much there is to learn from play! Play allows a child to explore and learn through their sensory systems, build relationships, explore their environments, understand how their body works in relation to the world, and then respond with well-practiced regulation skills.

Jaak Pankseep, a psychologist, identified behavioral circuits in the brain that include what he calls PLAY circuitry (Kestly, 2014). When we are in this circuitry, we feel safe, calm, and connected to others. Even when we experience fear or anxiety, we seek connection and calming from others. When we are fearful or anxious and able to connect with another person, we not only calm down, but also build connections in our brains. This cycle of *dysregulation* (over- or under-arousal; fight, flight, or freeze; disorganized nervous system) and *repair* (returning to a calm state) is what allows us to grow our capacity for self-regulation. When we feel connected to another person, we feel safe, so even in those scary moments we seek and benefit from relationship. For human infants, this process is essential to learning early self-regulation. We are not born with the ability to calm ourselves. Our nervous systems continue to develop and change throughout our lifespans, but during the early months and years of life, our brains are changing at an incredible speed, making the connections that are the foundation to all of our later development and learning. When we as caregivers use ourselves and our interactions to calm an infant, we label that "co-regulation."

The other side of this neurocircuitry is what Pankseep called the RAGE circuitry. In this circuitry, we are disconnected. We are unable to calm down with the help of others, and we are definitely unable to learn! When we are in this state, we can't reason, "use our words," or connect to the signals sent by our bodies. As therapists, parents, or teachers, helping a child (and ourselves) return to a calm state is the only thing we should be focused on in that moment. When our kids are in the middle of a meltdown, or what we might call a sensory assault, there is no punishment or behavioral strategy that is going to work. Kids aren't magically going to stop melting down or becoming dysregulated. This is when A SECRET may be the most helpful to give us a framework for staying organized through the chaos and to come out on the other side having actually built self-regulation skills!

To understand more about the PLAY circuitry and how it helps us build self-regulation, we can look at animal behavior. Let's think about a lioness and her cubs in the wild. She will spend a significant amount of time playing with her cubs, connecting and having fun but also setting limits. Instinctively, she knows when to stop, when her cubs have reached a level of arousal that is too much, or what we would call *too fast*. She will growl, maybe snap, or maybe just step away from the play as a sign that it is too much. She will *co-regulate* her cubs, keeping them in a "just-right state" or optimal level of arousal (see chart below). She recognizes that they are getting a little out of control with their play, and maybe it is getting more aggressive and less fun. She pulls them back from that high arousal or hyperarousal and back to a calm state, and by doing this she starts to teach them the real skills of self-regulation. When we are regulated, we are able to learn other important life skills like reading social cues, taking turns, impulse control, problem-solving, and empathy.

Figure 3.1

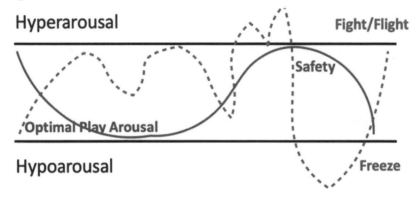

Figure 3.1. Arousal changes in play. Adapted from Kestly, 2014, page 23

What the lioness is doing through play is widening her pups' "optimal arousal" window during play, affecting not only play arousal, but also the window of arousal for the entire nervous system during other activities. Just like strengthening a muscle, practicing play arousal gives the young pups the opportunity to try and fail, and then to try again. It is the repetition within play that makes these connections strong. Just like with building muscle, we need a lot of practice to build the neural connections for self-regulation.

It is also essential to think about the optimal level of arousal play state as it relates to stress. Animals only play when there is no threat of danger. The lioness will enjoy this time with her cubs, but that fun stops the second she senses danger. As soon as she senses a predator in the area, play time is over. She moves out of that optimal level of arousal and into an adaptive state of fight or flight. We say adaptive because in this case, she needs to be in that state to have a heightened level of awareness so she can protect herself and her cubs. Her nervous system has adapted to a new danger she perceives. Her level of arousal raises, no longer happening just because the play was too much fun, but for protection. Her cubs learn to read her signs of alert and safety and her new social cues. They learn to pay attention to their surroundings and prepare to flee or fight to protect themselves when necessary. We will talk a little later about how this applies to people with SPD.

The Magic of Hide & Seek for Building Self-Regulation

Hide-and-seek is one of our favorite games for many reasons, but mostly for widening the window of optimal arousal. If you haven't played in many years, you may still be able to remember the level of excitement you felt when you were playing (and if you haven't played it recently, we highly recommend playing hide-and-seek soon!) We have to be careful and attune to our kids when playing, because hide-and-seek can create a state of *too-fast* arousal. In fact, many of our kids with SPD don't want to play hide-and-seek because it causes them too much anxiety. But if we pay attention to the child's signals, this game can be the perfect way to playfully combine the sympathetic (excitatory) and parasympathetic (inhibitory) nervous system responses and get into a wonderful state we call "flow" (Csikszentmihalyi, 2014), described in more detail later in this chapter. For kids with more regulatory challenges, a trusted adult must hide with them to closely watch their arousal changes and help them co-regulate, using proximity, facial gestures, voice volume, or other *Emotion Regulation* or *Relationship* strategies to let them know they are safe (see *Emotion Regulation* in chapter 11 and *Relationship* in chapter 10 for detailed discussion of strategies). Plus you'll have fun too! Now that you know how effective it is for children to 'work' on regulation using naturalistic authentic play with a partner (parent or therapist or older child), you can be genuinely playful and relax into a PLAY state with your child!

How Relationships Build Self-Regulation

When we start to learn about the science behind play, we can see the importance of relationship within every playful interaction. But we can't play all the time! Even in therapy, we have goals to reach that sometimes can't involve playful interactions. Throughout this book, we will give examples of *Emotion Regulation* and *Relationship* strategies, but here we want to discuss the *why*. Why should you spend time learning these strategies and incorporating them into your daily routines? Because our brains are built for connection! It is our experiences, especially our social interactions, that stimulate brain growth and connections, specifically the connections that allow us to learn to self-regulate or calm ourselves when we are stressed.

The area of our brain that allows us to connect with another person, have social interactions, and laugh with friends is the same area that adjusts our responses to stress. This area, called the *limbic system*, is the part of our brain that controls our emotions. Calm and meaningful interactions with another person, usually a caregiver, can provide the experiences that build healthy brain connections in this 'emotion center'. As those connections build, we gain more and more ability to regulate our own emotions, thus becoming able to stay calm when we are under stress. Without these connections, we have no ability to organize or manage our negative emotions, and that's when fear or anger may take over. As Dr. Daniel Siegel says, we flip our lids (Siegel & Bryson, 2012). We can't reason at this point, we can't "use our words." We need something or someone to break into our nervous system cycle and bring us back to a calm state. At this point, talking about feelings does not help because it's unlikely a child can access their powers of reasoning in that moment, but it usually does involve a true connection with a trusted caregiver, partner, or friend. Again, it is the person-to-person or brain-to-brain connection that allows us to come back to a calm state and to recognize and feel that we are safe. You could say we "sense" we are safe. And when we do that, our brain connections grow.

The *Relationship* and *Emotion Regulation* strategies that we offer in this book will help your child (and you!) build those connections.

So How Does All of This Relate to Our Kids with SPD?

When we understand the important individual differences in the nervous systems of our kids with SPD, we can explain the physiological challenges that accompany behavioral states. Then we (parents, teachers, or therapists) can begin to shift our view of the behaviors that we see. We understand that behaviors are actually nervous system responses to what the body interprets as a real-life threat.

Research shows that kids with SPD do not have the same brain connections or the same nervous system capacity as typically developing children (Miller, Reisman, Machintosh, & Simon, 2001, Chang et al., 2014; Davies & Gavin, 2007; Lane, Reynolds, Dumenci, 2012; Owen et al., 2013; Schaff et al., 2010). They are more easily stressed by their sensory environments, quickly leaving the state of optimal level of arousal and jumping into the fight or flight zone, When this occurs, they have less nervous system capacity for calming themselves. Our nervous systems allow us to move in and out of the optimal level of arousal and to create an internal sense of safety. Our sympathetic nervous system keeps us upregulated when we need to be alert, when we know there is a threat of danger, and when we might need to run or fight. If the threat doesn't occur, then our parasympathetic system, or downregulating system, helps us return to a state of calm.

When kids with SPD are in 'fight or flight' mode, they do not have the ability to calm down on command.

We might get frustrated and say, "Stop that right now" or "Act your age and calm down!" But in a state of over-arousal, there is no way their brain can "calm down." Kids need more support, both sensory supports and relationship supports, to build the connections needed to learn self-regulation. They need more *co-regulation* from us (*Relationship* or *Emotion Regulation*) to support and build parasympathetic nervous system (putting the brakes on sympathetic nervous system) capacities. And because they sense danger when their sensory systems are bombarded by too much input, when more is too much, the child becomes unable to adapt. They also need more sensory supports (*Sensory* or *Environment*) to break the upward spiral. In this way, providing this combination of strategies, we can support and build their sympathetic nervous system capacities.

How Does All of This Relate to Older Kids and Adults?

Play is a great way to build self-regulation skills, but we can learn self-regulation and build connections in other ways too. Science shows that when we are in *flow* (Csikszentmihalyi, 2014), we are in a similar state of optimal learning and arousal. This flow can come from true playfulness, but we don't see that play state often in teens or adults nearly often enough. So what does that look like for adolescents and adults? The play circuitry identified by Panksepp doesn't have to mean playing tag, cops and robbers, or hide and seek. We can also be in this circuitry when we are in flow, connected to another person, or even when doing a task. We can find flow in those moments when we are at the just-right arousal level, maybe through conversation, physical activities, group interactions, or through nature, poetry, or music. It is different for each person. In those moments, we are safe, calm, and hopefully finding ways to socially connect to others. Through those social connections or state of flow, we continuously build our capacity for regulation. Here are a few examples of ways to support flow and nervous system functioning in teens and adults using A SECRET:

Sensory	Relationship	Task
• Decreasing distractions • Calming or alerting music • Proprioceptive input through yoga or exercise	• Team sports • Group work • 1-on-1 time with parent, partner, coach, therapist, or friend	• Climbing • Playing a musical instrument • Painting, drawing, other art form • Hiking, running, spending time outside • Journaling • Singing

Conclusion

What About the Caregiver?

Now, don't think that we've forgotten about you! All of this applies to caregivers as well. Our nervous systems can be just as on-edge as our kids', especially if we have our own individual sensory differences. Even if we don't have SPD, heightened stress levels or anxiety can impact our nervous systems too, making it harder for us to calm down and co-regulate with our kids. So many of the same strategies, and certainly the structure of A SECRET, can help you pay attention to your own needs. Brain-to-brain connections help all of us improve our abilities to self-regulate. As parents or teachers, you need to find your own support systems and recognize your own sensory differences to be able to support your kids. We highly recommend finding a support group or support forum (there are more and more online options available). There is also a lot of science behind mindfulness strategies, showing that even a few minutes a day can build those brain connections and make you more able to support your sensational kid. So, as you read through this book and think about strategies, think of your how you might use each element of A SECRET to support yourself!

At first glance, A SECRET may seem complicated and can be overwhelming, but when we start by understanding the science behind it, we can take it one step at a time and learn to incorporate it into our daily lives. It is the process of using A SECRET that slowly shifts our view on behaviors, sensory reactivity, and playfulness. The process allows us to create more than just a sensory diet. With the science behind A SECRET, we learn to create a ***sensory lifestyle***!

For all of the reasons outlined in this chapter, we use A SECRET to frame our recommendations and strategies. Our own clinical research shows that parents and teachers find the structure of A SECRET helpful for carrying over some of our play- and relationship-based OT intervention techniques to home, school, and the larger community (Porter et al., submitted). We realize that we can't always play (but we wish we could ☺). Setting clear limits at home and at school is necessary for providing structure and predictability for our kids (that's where *Culture* and *Task* come in), but when we learn to let go of control in certain situations and to interact playfully with our kids (*Emotion Regulation*), we improve relationships (*Relationship*), teach social-emotional skills, and promote positive neurological development.

References

Chang, Y. S., Owen, J. P., Desai, S. S., Hill, S. S., Arnett, A. B., Harris, J., Marco, E., & Mukherjee, P. (2014). Autism and sensory processing disorders: shared white matter disruption in sensory pathways but divergent connectivity in social-emotional pathways. *PloS One, 9*(7), e103038.

Csikszentmihalyi, M. (2014). Toward a psychology of optimal experience. In *Flow and the Foundations of Positive Psychology* (pp. 209-226). Springer, Dordrecht.

Davies, P. L., & Gavin, W. J. (2007). Validating the diagnosis of sensory processing disorders using EEG technology. *American Journal of Occupational Therapy, 61*(2), 176-189.

Kestly, T. A. (2014). *The interpersonal neurobiology of play: Brain-building interventions for emotional well-being.* WW Norton & Company.

Lane, S. J., Reynolds, S., & Dumenci, L. (2012). Sensory overresponsivity and anxiety in typically developing children and children with autism and attention deficit hyperactivity disorder: cause or coexistence? *American Journal of Occupational Therapy, 66*(5), 595-603.

Miller, L. J., Reisman, J. E., McIntosh, D. N., & Simon, J. (2001). An ecological model of sensory modulation: Performance of children with fragile X syndrome, autistic disorder, attention-deficit/hyperactivity disorder, and sensory modulation dysfunction. *Understanding the Nature of Sensory Integration with Diverse Populations,* 57-88.

Owen, J. P., Marco, E. J., Desai, S., Fourie, E., Harris, J., Hill, S. S., ... & Mukherjee, P. (2013). Abnormal white matter microstructure in children with sensory processing disorders. *Neuroimage: Clinical, 2,* 844-853.

Pajareya, K., & Nopmaneejumruslers, K. (2012). A one-year prospective follow-up study of a DIR/Floortime™ parent training intervention for preschool children with autistic spectrum disorders. *Journal of the Medical Association of Thailand*, 95(9), 1184.

Porter, L., Lane, S., Sweeney, J., Demchick, B., Mullens, P., & Kearney, B., (submitted) Learning Needs During a Group Parent-training with Parents of Children with Sensory Over-responsivity: A Mixed Methods Study.

Schaaf, R. C., Benevides, T. W., Blanche, E., Brett-Green, B. A., Burke, J., Cohn, E., ... & Parham, D. (2010). Parasympathetic functions in children with sensory processing disorder. *Frontiers in Integrative Neuroscience*, 4, 4.

Siegel, D. J. (2012). *Pocket guide to interpersonal neurobiology: An Integrative Handbook of the Mind* (*Norton Series on Interpersonal Neurobiology*). WW Norton & Company.

Siegel, D. J., & Bryson, T. P. (2012). *The Whole-Brain Child: 12 Revolutionary Strategies to Nurture Your Child's Developing Mind*. Bantam.

Solomon, R., Van Egeren, L. A., Mahoney, G., Huber, M. S. Q., & Zimmerman, P. (2014). PLAY Project Home Consultation intervention program for young children with autism spectrum disorders: a randomized controlled trial. *Journal of Developmental and Behavioral Pediatrics*, 35(8), 475.

Thelen, E. (2005). Dynamic systems theory and the complexity of change. *Psychoanalytic Dialogues*, 15(2), 255-283.

CHAPTER 4

FROM THEORY TO ACTION: ESSENTIAL COMPONENTS OF ASSESSMENT

How to Get Started and What to Ask

As therapists trained in sensory processing and integration, it makes sense that we prioritize the assessment of sensory processing and integration challenges. But we know that to understand the whole child, we must examine more than just sensory functions. It is our perspective as authors of this book that while sensory information is critical, information about motor abilities, relationships, engagement, and regulation is equally important.

Evaluation is the beginning of treatment. The focus is usually related to a question such as whether there are interventions appropriate to increase success, enhance skill development, and improve self-regulation. For children with developmental or medical issues, there is more interest in determining strengths and limitations and in suggesting particular enrichment activities.

Certainly many different sorts of questions are asked, so there are many purposes of evaluation. It is essential to make sure you know the reason a person needs the evaluation before beginning the process. Remember, we are interested in knowing the child's 'best' performance, not his 'test' performance. Try to put the child and family at ease as you start. Always greet the child and the parent, attuning to the child's individual differences from the moment you meet them in the waiting room. Putting them at east might mean having the child sit on the floor on a ball to complete the evaluation. Maybe it means having the parent sit in the testing room with the child. Maybe it means taking lots of water breaks or bathroom breaks. Maybe the child is used to wearing a weighted vest or having a weighted blanket on his lap, or maybe you show the child the "fun room" (OT gym or outdoor play space if you have one) and tell them that as soon as they are done with these games, they will be able to go to the play space and choose what they want to play on. Of course, any changes you make to the test's standardization instruction should be noted in the written report, which you might document as follows: "The instructions for administering a standardized scale were modified to obtain the child's best performance. The scores obtained represent their 'best' performance in a quiet space, with a one-on-one relationship with an examiner experienced in coaxing high performance from children. *Suzy* might perform differently in her natural environment. The testing environment was altered in the following ways..." Document all environmental or testing modifications.

Often a parent will bring a child in for an evaluation without a clear reason for the testing. Meeting privately with the parent is well worth the time for an evaluator. In order to answer the right questions, it is essential that we understand parents' and teachers' concerns before we perform an assessment. Whenever possible, we recommend spending time with the parent to obtain a thorough developmental history, including a story of how the child functions in their natural setting. This also provides an excellent opportunity to develop a strong relationship with the parent from the beginning. This may be impossible in some settings, but even if it is a conversation on the phone, it is helpful.

"Good is the enemy of great" (Collins, 2001). This is the first sentence of one of our favorite books. What does that mean? While it seems somewhat odd, the intention is to remind readers that trying to be *good* may lead you to pause when you feel it is *good enough*. This may lead to stopping before you get to great. An evaluation that will satisfy the good enough criteria is rarely *great*. When we work with children with disabilities and their families, what they are seeking is the best, the very best evaluation possible. A *good* evaluation is rarely *good enough* for our children and their families, who are often in crisis. *Good enough* is not enough for them. Being a service provider and offering your specialty to others is a great responsibility. It is more than a job. Lives depend on accurate reading of a child's strengths and limitations, goals and sorrows, attempts to perform and resistance to excellence. So each new evaluation presents a new challenge to you.

When you are asked to identify the root of a child's challenges, a huge burden is placed on your shoulders. This burden should include, most importantly, pointing out the child's strengths. The questions you have to answer can be incredibly complex, and the answers are always multifactorial. You have the awesome responsibility of providing a family with feedback that may well affect the child's life forever. The answer(s) for a teen or adult may, if asked correctly, create an environment leading to a life of value and success.

This chapter will not provide you with answers to your evaluation questions. One of the most frequent questions we get when we teach seminars is "What is the best test?" There is no "best test"; the question is "What is the best test to [insert a purpose here]?" Some more specific questions might be "What is your opinion of the best test in a school situation to assess a child's fine motor skill? What is your opinion of the best test to measure readiness to read? What is the best test to predict success in kindergarten?" Or more broadly, "I am concerned about my child's attention abilities. What is the best way to predict attention?"

If there is not a test designed that has normative data for the specific challenges of a child you are seeing, you should be clear with your client that you are using an alternative method to gather clinical observations. The results should include your expert opinion AND the parents' expert opinion, rather than standardized test scores. Parent-report measures are an essential piece of the puzzle when combined with clinical expertise and observation. The evaluation is a process of engaging with a new client, understanding their gifts, and assessing what factors affect them and those around them.

It is your responsibility to be honest about evaluation findings, and that is not always easy, especially if you are a new therapist. It becomes easier as we have more experience to draw from. We can say, "I have seen several (dozens? hundreds?) of children who have had similar test results and, in my experience, those families were happy with their child's attentional improvements at school, their improved relationship with their child, fewer outbreaks of temper tantrums..." If you are lucky enough to work in a system with other professionals, you can expand your "data" to include a large range of children seen in your setting.

Goal Attainment Scaling

In this book, we are not going into great detail with the evaluation of sensory challenges. It would take a whole book devoted to that topic to cover it well. However, two aspects of evaluation are important to mention in more detail: 1) Goal Attainment Scaling (GAS) and 2) Impact Statements, as they relate closely to using A SECRET for goal development and treatment planning.

It is essential for the entire team (parent, therapist, teacher, other healthcare professionals, extended family) to understand a child's goals and to know that goals are set based on the parent's priorities. We strongly suggest you use Goal Attainment Scaling to achieve this. We have found that the time you spend making your GAS goals is well worth the effort. There are many advantages to using GAS, but the most important is getting all team members on the same page. Parents, teachers, and therapists work together to create meaningful goals, so everyone is focused on the same outcome.

Our team at the STAR Center was the first to conduct a randomized controlled trial using GAS as an outcome measure (Miller, Coll, & Schoen, 2007). We found that OT was effective in helping children achieve many outcomes, but the most significant finding was change in GAS scores, demonstrating that GAS is a sensitive and effective outcome measure. Now, several other researchers have replicated this finding with children with autism spectrum disorder (Pfeiffer et al., 2011; Schaaf et al., 2014). This validates the importance of GAS for research purposes, and also for clinical use.

GAS is a method of designing a few (3–5) key goals for your client so you can evaluate changes based on these *individualized* goals, rather than expecting changes on standardized scales based on group norms. Group standardized scales may find changes over a longer period of time, and groups should comprise at least 30 people in each treatment type you are studying with approximately 10 subjects in each of the age groupings for which you intend the findings to be useful. We recommend treatment whenever possible (several months of treatment, once a day) for an individual student.

Advantages of GA Scaling

Goal attainment scaling has a number of advantages, including forming a partnership with the family from the start of the therapy process. Goals are created with the family during an interview with the therapist. The therapist will ask specific questions to support the writing of goals that are specific, measurable, and most importantly, focused on the parents' concerns. Because of this process of goal development, changes are more meaningful to the family. Researchers have been using GAS as an outcome measure for decades and most recently in the study of OT outcomes. GAS is an excellent outcome measure because it has been found to be sensitive to small increments of change.

In our research with Ellen Cohn, PhD, (Miller, Cohn, Tickle-Degnen, 2000) regarding the hopes of parents for therapy outcomes, we found four consistent themes. Four child-focused and two parent-focused themes related to parents' hopes for therapy outcomes for their children with challenges in sensory processing:

Child-centered themes:
- Improve social participation
- Improve self-regulation
- Increase confidence and self-esteem
- Increase specific abilities in performance areas

Parent-Centered Themes:
- Provide the parent with a "toolbox" (3–4 specific strategies) to support children at home/school
- Provide parental support around the 'reality' of the diagnosis and for the difficulties inherent in living with a child who has a 'hidden handicap'

How to Administer GAS

To determine GAS goals, you first ask parents open-ended questions. For example:

- Tell me about Shane. What kinds of things does he enjoy? What things about him do you especially enjoy? What are his gifts?
- Tell me about Shane's abilities in daily self-care activities
- What have you noticed about Shane's [fill in with an area of parents' concern] that particularly worries you?
- What is school like for Shane?
- What are your expectations and/or hopes for therapy?

You might say to parents, "Let's pretend therapy is over and you are deciding whether treatment was successful. What are a few changes that would make you say, 'Yes, that was worth the time, money and effort we put into it'?"

Writing goals: From the information you receive in this open-ended manner, you and the parent *together* define the child's goals from treatment. Here are some examples from Shane:

Goal #1:

After intervention for 30 sessions, Shane will increase the time he can engage in and enjoy free play with his twin brother without melting down.

MARKER: The amount of time Shane can play with his twin brother without conflict in a specific environment (such as after snack following return from school to home).

There are a multitude of contexts you might choose, such as on a weekend morning when the boys get up and play together while they wait for parents, or in the afternoon after lunch but before they work on homework. It doesn't matter what you choose, but define the parameter well so it can be replicated by another researcher.

CURRENT PERFORMANCE: Shane's mother must always provide assistance to Shane and his twin brother during play for peace and fun to be exhibited.

GA Item #1:

After intervention for 30 sessions, Shane will be able to play with his brother for 5 minutes without Mom's or Dad's assistance.

-2	Shane cannot play peacefully with his brother ever, no matter how much physical or verbal support his parents offer
-1	Shane will play calmly with his brother for 5 minutes with a parent mediating every step of the way both physically and verbally
0	Shane will play with his brother for 5 minutes with Mom's or Dad's *physical assistance* the whole time to 'keep the peace'
1	Shane will play with his brother for 5 minutes with parent's *verbal* reminders only
2	Shane will play with his brother in a regulated way for 5 minutes without Mom's or Dad's assistance

Goal #2:

After intervention for 30 sessions, Shane will increase his ability to eat a meal with his brother without parental assistance in keeping the boys calm.

MARKER: The amount of assistance Shane needs to eat a meal with his brother

CURRENT PERFORMANCE: Shane's mother or father must always provide full time assistance to Shane and his twin brother during meals for nonconflictual behaviors to be exhibited

-2	Shane never eats lunch independently with his twin without conflict
-1	Shane eats lunch independently with his brother for 5 minutes without sibling conflict
0	Shane eats lunch independently with his brother for 10 minutes without parental intervention
1	Shane eats lunch independently with his brother for 15 minutes without parental intervention
2	Shane eats lunch independently with his brother for 20 minutes without parental intervention to eliminate conflicts

Considerations When Writing Good GA Items:

- Must be measurable (You can't say "Shane gets better at playing with his brother"]
- Based on parents' priorities (You wouldn't say "Shane's range of motion is improved by 20 degrees in his hips")
- Does not use percentage of time as an outcome. It is essentially impossible to measure a percentage of time. (You wouldn't say "Shane plays for 10 minutes with brother independently 25% of the time.")
- Will be better if written by experienced therapist who can make an educated guess about what is realistic to achieve in a certain treatment duration
- Helpful to note what the time limit is to meet this goal
- Only change one marker in each goal. For example, you wouldn't include time limit, the, amount of assistance needed, and skill in performing task in the same goal. (You would not say, "Over time, Shane will improve in playing with his brother nicely and independently.")

A GA item is just a *marker of change*. It is not a good choice to evaluate quality of life changes. In Shane's example, the items are markers of Shane's ability to relate to his brother in a regulated manner. These items do not include the whole span of his life. The OT is not trying to measure a change in the child's 'life's performance.' The item is looking at small increments of change that are markers of larger quality of life issues. These markers can ask questions such as:

- How many units changed?
- In what locations was a change noted?
- How much assistance was needed for the child to accomplish the task?
- For how long was the change observed?

It is important to gather specific information regarding frequency, duration, or intensity of behaviors or functional areas of concern.

Frequency:
- How often does your child melt down?
- How many days a week is there an aggressive outburst?
- How many times a day (or week) does your child lose their homework?

Duration:
- How long do meltdowns last?
- How long does your child sit at the dinner table?
- How long does it take for them to fall asleep?

Intensity:
- Describe a typical meltdown. Does your child hit, bite, or yell?
- How much support does your child need to go to bed at night? Do you need to be in bed with them?
- Please provide details about your child's food restrictions. How many foods do they eat? Will they sit down at the table when unfamiliar or non-preferred foods are present?

Common Errors in Writing GA Items for GA Scales:

1. Includes more than one type of measurable objective

   Example: Follows two-step picture schedule with assistance from teacher 25% of time

2. Does not define a measurable amount of change

   Example: Plays well with brother (what is "well"?)

3. Is not based on parents' priorities

   Example: Has increased stability as evidenced by ability increasing balance (The parents are concerned about play on playground, inability to join with others his age in soccer, etc. They would not put it in terms of increased stability.)

Impact Statements

Another recommendation for evaluation is to improve the clarity and specificity of treatment objectives by writing impact statements in your evaluations. These will identify the primary challenges related to SPD sub-patterns and relate them directly to parents' concerns. A good impact statement reframes a child's functional, social, and participation challenges by helping parents identify the root or sensory processing foundation of functional concerns. Rather than focusing on scores, an impact statement links the parents' areas of concern directly to the OT assessment, and then to intervention. Here are a few examples:

Impact of Ryder's postural challenges on being accident-prone: Postural control is the foundation for gross motor, fine motor, and oral motor actions, which require good motor control. Without a stable core body, performing refined actions is difficult. Ryder plays roughly with others and has difficulty judging appropriate force, such as when throwing or kicking a ball. When moving, especially when excited, Ryder often uses more force than necessary, resulting in accidents including hitting or crashing into others. Ryder's poor postural control affects his ability to engage in physical play, and he appears clumsy, awkward, and accident-prone, affecting the other children's willingness to play with him.

Impact of sensory discrimination challenges on participation in novel or multi-step tasks: Walter demonstrates difficulty interpreting sensory information from his tactile and proprioceptive systems (touch and muscle/joint force), as well as his auditory and visual systems. Walter participates well during the initial assessment but demonstrates difficulty with complex motor tasks such as the catching, throwing, and jumping items on the test. Parent report measures also indicate challenges with interpreting sensory information.

In order to perform novel and multi-step tasks, it is necessary to register and interpret information from all of our senses. For children with sensory discrimination challenges, it may be difficult to interpret input from one sense at a time, and even more difficult to integrate input from multiple senses. This is likely playing a significant role in Walter's ability to follow directions and participate in group activities.

Impact of poor sensory modulation on peer interactions and self-regulation: Sensory modulation is the ability to take in sensory input while regulating the degree, intensity, or nature of response to the input. Given accurate modulation of sensations, children can grade and adapt to differing and unexpected sensations while maintaining an optimal level of arousal. At this optimal level, children are able to perform daily tasks and adapt to challenges while remaining regulated. Rosa demonstrates sensory craving behaviors, such as becoming overly excited with movement, constantly seeking movement, touching people or objects, and putting things in her mouth. Being unable to modulate the intensity or duration of input means that Rosa is frequently functioning outside of her "optimal level of arousal." When her nervous system is unorganized, she may have difficulty interacting with peers, particularly on the playground or in other loud environments. She may seek sensory input to organize herself but does not recognize when she has had "enough." She may have frequent outbursts or demonstrate aggressive behavior when she is out of her optimal level of arousal.

We believe that the addition of goal attainment scaling and impact statements adds significant depth to the OT evaluation. These tools help us connect and build trust with families and give us an opportunity to listen to families' stories. When used together, GAS and impact statements put families at an advantage, providing insight into the therapy process and an understanding of how SPD impacts their child's daily functioning. From the very beginning, we are setting the stage for success.

References

Cohn, E., Miller, L. J., & Tickle-Degnen, L. (2000). Parental hopes for therapy outcomes: Children with sensory modulation disorders. *American Journal of Occupational Therapy*, 54(1), 36-43.

Collins, Jim. (2001). *Good to Great*. HarperCollins Publishers. NY.

Miller, L. J., Coll, J. R., & Schoen, S. A. (2007). A randomized controlled pilot study of the effectiveness of occupational therapy for children with sensory modulation disorder. *American Journal of Occupational Therapy*, 61(2), 228-238.

Pfeiffer, B. A., Koenig, K., Kinnealey, M., Sheppard, M., & Henderson, L. (2011). Effectiveness of sensory integration interventions in children with autism spectrum disorders: A pilot study. *American Journal of Occupational Therapy*, 65(1), 76-85.

Schaaf, R. C., Benevides, T., Mailloux, Z., Faller, P., Hunt, J., Van Hooydonk, E., ... & Kelly, D. (2014). An intervention for sensory difficulties in children with autism: A randomized trial. *Journal of Autism and Developmental Disorders*, 44(7), 1493-1506.

CHAPTER 5

ATTUNEMENT

A = Attunement

How do we use *Attunement* to support regulation and success?

A SECRET							
Challenge Area	Attunement	Sensation	Emotion Regulation	Culture	Relation-ship	Environment	Task

In the first edition of this book, the A in A SECRET stood for *Attention*. Based on our experiences with hundreds of children, families, and therapists, we realized that there was something deeper than attention. We also had many families and therapists tell us that learning to attune, or attend and respond to emotions (both their child's and their own!) was one of the more important takeaways from therapy. So, we have modified A SECRET slightly to reflect this essential element. You will still see us referring to attunement as a strategy under *Emotion Regulation* and *Relationship*, but this chapter will focus on the importance of attuning to emotional and physical responses. We'll discuss caregivers attuning to our own and our children's emotional reactions and building these abilities in our children. This chapter will also cover how we help children attend to and recognize their reactions to emotions, which is foundational to emotion regulation.

Attunement describes how reactive a person is to another's emotional needs and moods. A person who is well attuned will respond with appropriate language and behaviors based on someone else's emotional state. *Attunement* is the state of being aware of the feelings and reactivity of another person. It is the process by which we form relationships. Dr. Dan Siegel says, "When we *attune* with others, we allow our own internal state to shift, to come to resonate with the inner world of another" (2017). To bring into accord, harmony, or sympathetic relationship, we can adjust as such: The mother was attuned to her daughter's moods and feelings with little effort, as she automatically shifted into a supportive role as her daughter began to feel anxious around certain friends.

Attunement is one of the most important skills that parents and teachers can have. Sometimes our children's behaviors are difficult to understand. When they have automatic fearful reactions in situations that seem safe to us but unsafe to them, it may take a great deal of restraint to stay calm (see Chapters 2 and 3). When we are attuned to our children, we are able to recognize when they are in fight or flight or the *Regulate* level, and this can help us stay calm and offer co-regulation.

Here's an example:

Heather is 13 years old. She has been begging her mom for days to let her go to the community pool without supervision. Her mom, Sally, is worried, because although Heather is a good swimmer, her judgment leaves a lot to be desired. She is emotionally immature, and her mom feels she needs to 'pave the way' to peaceful interactions with other children her age. Last week at the pool, Heather was hanging out with a group of friends when all of a sudden, her mom heard a loud shriek. When she looked toward the scream, she saw that Heather was upset because one of the boys had splashed her in fun. Heather was upset because she was not expecting to be splashed, and it set off a 'danger' signal in the part of her brain responsible for quickly processing and expressing emotions, called the amygdala (pronounced *uh-MIG-duh-luh*).

Development of Reasoning/Prefrontal Cortex

When our kids are upset, melting down, or "making bad choices," we often want to reason with them. We might ask them to use their words or expect them to be able to "make good choices," but it is important to understand that their brains have not developed the ability to reason. In many cases, the prefrontal cortex, the reasoning part of the brain, isn't fully developed until the late 20s! In fact, the neurological development of reasoning is one of the main jobs of adolescence. The process is so involved that the period of adolescence is now considered to be as long as ages 12–26 (Siegel, 2015). When we can attune to our children's (or teenagers') individual differences and use the elements of A SECRET to help them regulate, we are actually helping to build neurological connections and reasoning at the *Evaluate* and *Respond* level (see chapter 2).

It is the amygdala's job to react quickly to keep you safe. If Heather were hiking and sees a snake in the path, it would be appropriate for her amygdala to fire up an immediate reaction, and she might give an immediate shrill scream and freeze in place. That reaction would be appropriate to the context and circumstance of seeing a snake. However, at the pool, playing with her friends, it was an overreaction to being splashed, especially in fun. People say Heather is "high-strung" and that this sort of interaction happens frequently. If her mother is there, she can gently come to the rescue and make a comment that will soothe Heather while explaining to Jose that some people need a fun comment to prepare them for the stimulation. Sally quickly moved over to the kids and said, "Heather is a bit sensitive to unexpected splashing, Jose. How could you have warned her the splash was coming?"

Jose is a good kid who meant no harm. He was, in fact, surprised at Heather's strong reaction. "I guess I could have warned her," he said. I could have asked her if she wanted to play splash with me." "Exactly," replied Sally. Heather, meanwhile, was standing to the side, getting herself calm. It was just a quick, little event, and luckily, she knew Jose well and generally liked him. The whole little event only took a minute and blew over quickly before the little mismatch between Heather and Jose could become a big deal and spoil the day.

Heather's mom was so used to rescuing her daughter that it barely registered how important her role was. At the same time, Heather was both grateful to her mom and irritated that her mom had stepped in. Awkward... And thus, the situation left Heather feeling a little exasperated with her mom. But Sally was uniquely and wonderfully *attuned* to Heather's emotional states and incredibly well-suited to paving the way for Heather. While the experience only lasted a minute, because of her mom's attunement to her daughter, it blew over quickly, and her mom left the teens to finish their own repair and went back to playing with her younger child.

In this example, Sally is almost hypervigilant. For 13 years, she's had to attune to Heather's sensory differences to try to avoid meltdowns or reactions due to sensory assaults. At 13, Heather may be ready to return to OT to focus on attunement to her own emotional responses. An OT could help her tune in to her reactions and understand where they are coming from. She may also be ready to learn strategies to support self-regulation skills and use A SECRET to problem-solve her own solutions.

In this example, it's also likely that Sally has some heightened sensory reactions of her own. After years of being on alert and being ready to respond to and support Heather, she probably hasn't paid attention to her own needs. What happens to Sally's arousal level when Heather's amygdala is firing? What strategies does she have to support herself so she can co-regulate Heather? When using A SECRET in this example, an OT can help Sally attune to her own sensory differences and emotional reactions.

Supporting Caregivers in Attuning to Their Own Emotional Responses

Of course pediatric occupational therapy (OT) is focused on the child, but OTs know that the best way to support a child is by supporting the entire family. We call this Family-Centered Care or using a family-systems approach. It is considered best practice in most healthcare professions to address concerns of the whole family. We can't look at a child in isolation, especially when we are using a relationship-based approach. If self-regulation starts from connections between an infant and their caregiver, and continues through co-regulation as children develop, we must look at those interactions and relationships as part of our therapy. So, these strategies are focused on the caregiver. Consider these strategies as ways to build attunement to your own emotional reactions and sensory differences:

- Consider asking your child's OT if you can fill out a sensory questionnaire for yourself
- Begin to pay attention to the strategies you use to calm yourself down
- Keep a journal logging your sensory triggers and your supports

- Which sensory systems are more triggering for you?
- What time of day are you most stressed and likely to react strongly?
- Do you feel differently on days that you are able to exercise or connect with a friend?
- Use your child's self-regulation OT strategies on yourself
  - Tools like The Self-regulation Alert Program®, The Incredible 5-Point Scale, and The Zones of Regulation® are helpful for anybody, child or adult
  - Use these tools along with your child. Not only will you model for your child, but you'll also build skills for yourself
- Identify self-regulation strategies that work for you and build them into your day
  - Even a few minutes of daily mindfulness increases the connections in our brain and improves self-regulation (Goleman & Davidson, 2017; Siegel & Solomon, 2020)
  - We know mindfulness doesn't work for everyone. What works for you?
    - Yoga
    - Running
    - Caregiver support groups
    - Walk or hike
    - Phone call or visit with friends
    - Taking a bath

- If you don't have time to fit a new routine into your day, what about just trying to slow down and be in the moment?
  - Use a red light to practice deep breathing
  - Take 1 minute to pay attention to 5 things you can see, 4 things you can hear, 3 things you can touch, 2 things you can smell, and 1 thing you can taste

The point is to attune to yourself! What are your strengths (what helps you regulate) and what are your challenges (when do you dysregulate)? Paying attention to these things will help you...and with help, you help your child! ☺

Important to this event was the short conversation Sally and Heather had that night in the privacy of Heather's bedroom, as Sally was giving her the routine backrub which gave them some private time every day and a chance to briefly process any issues or successes that had happened that day. "Good night, my big girl," said Sally. "Night, Mom," replied Heather. "Anything you want to talk about tonight?" asked Sally. Heather thought about it for a few minutes. She was pulled back and forth by her need for independence and her reliance on her mom. It was a good private time for them to communicate. Maybe it was time for Heather to tell Mom she was getting too old to be rescued. What should she do?

Attunement Strategies

As you read through this section, you will see that many of the strategies here could also fit under *Emotion Regulation* or *Relationship* ⟲ , and we've done that for a reason. We believe that these elements and strategies are so essential to supporting regulation and success that we want to repeat them here in this book! It is also essential to remember that we are all different. Because of our individual differences, not all strategies will work for any particular person. And what works one day might not work the next. Don't give up! Remember that A SECRET was created just for this very reason. We're not just giving a static list of strategies, and attunement is the key! When you are attuned, you will know when to shift strategies, interactions, routines, and any of the other elements. ⟲

What will help you become even more attuned than you already are?

- Take time to **observe** your child in different contexts or environments. By doing so, you can learn to recognize their triggers or challenges, and their preferences for regulating.
- Work with your child's OT to **learn** about your child's individual sensory differences.
- Remember that your child may be using some strategies that may not fit our social norms. For instance, if your child is over-responsive to visual input, it may be very overwhelming to make eye contact. Instead of pushing your child to make eye contact, consider alternatives.
  - Can your child give a quick wave instead of making eye contact?

- Can you create a script or a few words to use in social situations to explain your child's sensory preferences?
- Can you help your child make a *safe* plan for social interactions?
- **Allow for individual differences.** We all have ways to calm our nervous systems. For some people, flapping their hands or rocking side to side is what they need to do to stay connected in unfamiliar environments. Work with your child to acknowledge and support their sensory needs.
- Recognize that your child may not be able to participate in certain tasks when they are stressed or when their arousal levels are high.
  - For example, when you're late for school and everyone is rushed, this is probably not the time to insist that your child tie their shoes independently.
  - They will need more help and more co-regulation when they are melting down. This is not the time to ask them to use words to describe how they are feeling or to use a new self-regulation strategy to calm down.
- Create opportunities (when your child is calm) to work together on awareness of emotions and changes in level of alertness or arousal level.
- Model awareness of your own emotional responses and self-regulation needs.
- It can be very helpful to talk about your own issues within the context of a discussion with your child about their strategies. That can provide a bridge for your child to talk about their strategies and worries.

Reflection

Take some time to consider the following questions. Reflection is one of the best ways to build attunement to ourselves and to others.

What strategies does your child use to try to regulate their nervous system?

_____

_____

_____

_____

_____

_____

_____

_____

How do you respond when these strategies don't fit social norms or expectations?

_____

_____

_____

_____

_____

_____

_____

_____

What tools do you use to help increase your child's awareness of their emotions? How does your child respond to these tools? When is your child able to engage with these tools? How do you know when it may not be the time to push these tools?

_____

_____

_____

_____

_____

_____

_____

_____

What sensory tools do you use to regulate your nervous system? Which sensory systems are most calming or regulating for you? (Touch, vision, taste, smell, sound, movement, or heavy work/proprioception)

_____

_____

_____

_____

_____

_____

_____

_____

How do you build these strategies or tools into your daily routines? If you don't have them built into your day, what's one small step you could take today?

_____

_____

_____

_____

_____

_____

_____

_____

Below are some examples of *Attunement* strategies that use what we call process points. These examples will not fit every child or family but should be used as a guide. The reflection above should help you think about building attunement and using attunement skills to support yourself and your child. Use the reflection to think about *Attunement* process points that will work for you and your child.

A SECRET

Challenge Area	Attunement	Sensation	Emotion Regulation	Culture	Relationship	Environment	Task
	Work with an OT to identify your child's sensory differences	⊙					
	Pay attention to your own sensory differences	⊙					
	Keep a list of activities that support your child's arousal regulation		⊙				⊙
	Closely observe your child in new environments. Watch for sensory triggers	⊙	⊙			⊙	
	Closely observe your child in new environments. What type of sensory input do they seek for comfort or regulation?	⊙	⊙				
	What happens to your own arousal level when your child is having a meltdown?	⊙	⊙				
	What adaptive (helpful) strategies do you use to stay calm when your child is melting down?		⊙	⊙			
	What habits do you have when your child is melting down?			⊙			
	Pay attention to the times when you and your child are most connected				⊙		

101

References

Goleman, D., & Davidson, R. J. (2017). *Altered Traits: Science Reveals How Meditation Changes Your Mind, Brain, and Body*. Penguin.

McKee, L. G., Parent, J., Zachary, C. R., & Forehand, R. (2018). Mindful parenting and emotion socialization practices: Concurrent and longitudinal associations. *Family Process*, 57(3), 752-766.

Kabat-Zinn, J. (2006). *Mindfulness for Beginners*. Louisville, CO. Sounds True.

Siegel, D. J. (2015). *Brainstorm: The Power and Purpose of the Teenage Brain*. Penguin.

Siegel, D. J., & Solomon, M. F. (2020). *Mind, Consciousness, and Well-Being (Norton Series on Interpersonal Neurobiology)*. WW Norton & Company.

CHAPTER 6

SENSATION

S = Sensation

How do we use Sensation to support success?

A SECRET							
Challenge Area	Attunement	Sensation	Emotion Regulation	Culture	Relation-ship	Environment	Task

In chapters 2 and 3, we provided an in-depth overview of sensation and the basics of the neurological underpinnings of how sensation affects regulation. We don't need to think about sensation on this level to appreciate how we can use it to support children with sensory challenges, or anyone for that matter! However, it is important to understand that sensation plays an essential role at all brain levels, from perception and regulation up to the higher levels of discrimination and response.

Sensation is essential to every aspect of our daily functioning, from early development to self-care, academics, and self-regulation.

In this chapter, we will provide general strategies for using *Sensation* to support your child's success. We will also discuss how *Sensation* may challenge your child and get in the way of success, while simultaneously contributing to dysregulation. Remember, when you recognize both sensory strengths and challenges, you will be able to use *Sensation* to help your child thrive. Sensory tools are essential to supporting kids with SPD, but they do not work in isolation. That's why the other elements of A SECRET are so important! A sensory strategy that works in one setting (e.g., in the classroom), may not work in another context (e.g., at bedtime). But when *you* know the secret, you can use the elements to help your child find success wherever and whenever they have difficulty.

What Are Your Individual Sensory Differences?

We all have what we call individual sensory differences. It can be helpful to start by bringing awareness to your own sensory differences. What are your sensory supports or areas of strength? What sensations are bothersome for you? Are you more bothered by certain sensations when you are stressed, tired, hungry, or frustrated? Becoming aware of your own sensory differences may help you become more attuned to your child's sensory needs. Consider the following questions:

- What sensory tools do you use to help you calm down (e.g., listening to music, exercising, curling up under a heavy blanket, getting a massage, chewing gum, pacing, fidgeting)?
- What sensations are most irritating to you (e.g., loud noises, tight clothes, certain smells, crowded or visually overwhelming spaces)?
- Is there one sensory system that is most calming for you (e.g., tactile, auditory, proprioceptive)?

Spend some time paying attention to your own sensory differences. Jot down a list of your preferred sensations and those that are challenging for you.

The Fuel Tank Analogy

The fuel tank analogy can be used to understand differences in sensory modulation (sensory over- or under-responsivity). This analogy is sometimes used to help people visualize their responses to sensory input. As helpful as this analogy can be in terms of general association with what is happening in a child's brain, it is intended to be a simple explanation that does not come close to describing the intricacies of the human brain. We already have enough data to know that the actual mechanisms of SPD are complex and will likely be known as even more complicated once they are fully understood.

Like cars, nervous systems vary in size, the type of "fuel" needed, the quantity of "fuel" used for highest performance, and the amount of fuel needed to fill up the gas tank. Individuals' needs for sensory input can be compared to the varying needs of car engines. Think of the sensory input that our bodies need to function as if the sensory input were fuel for your car. The fuel (sensation) is sent to your brain through neural pathways the way gasoline is pumped to your car's engine. Individuals need different amounts and types of "fuel" to function well (Figure 6.1).

Figure 6.1

Figure 6.1. Modulation states for sensory over-responsivity (left) and sensory under-responsivity (right)

Some people have nervous systems that seem "more sensitive" and require less "fuel" to evoke an intense response. These individuals have smaller "gas tanks," so they "fill up" with only a little fuel. Often their tank fills so quickly and their capacity is so small that the "gas" overflows. This would be like a sensory over-responsive person; the overflow might manifest as a temper tantrum or an aggressive or anxious event. Individuals with small "gas tanks "may have lower sensory thresholds and may become overloaded by sensation easily, often feeling threatened, anxious, or worried. Children with sensory over-responsivity exhibit discomfort and/or fear and try to escape from sensory stimulation that seems perfectly normal to typically developing children, such as a noisy cafeteria, a movie theater, or a sports arena.

In comparison, other people have nervous systems that seem "less sensitive" than others' and require "more fuel" to function maximally or even to notice what is going on around them. The "gas tank" in individuals with sensory under-responsivity is deep and large and requires an enormous quantity of gas to reach a "full" state. When less than "full," an under-responsive child appears lethargic and/or unaware of their environment and the surrounding sensory messages.

Attuning or paying attention to your child's sensory differences will help you identify when their fuel tank needs attention. Using the strategies in this chapter (along with other ⟳ elements of A SECRET) will help you create a sensory lifestyle for your child and your family.

Josh's Story

Josh is a brilliant 5-year-old boy going on 35. He was referred to us because he couldn't get along with his classmates. He was the only child of a father who was a federal judge and a mother who was the CEO of a Fortune 500 company. Josh was creative and curious, but he also had many challenges. One of the main concerns was that whenever his kindergarten classroom got the least bit loud, he burst into tears and threw tantrums. After many weeks of treatment, his therapist, Renee, finally arranged an opportunity for both the parents and Josh to be home at a time when we could visit his home and school. The light bulb went on!

Josh's kindergarten occurred in an open classroom. The children decided which station they wanted to work at and played there until a bell was rung, and they could choose to either move or stay at that station. Transitions were a time of chaos; the kids were loud, and the teachers moved from station to station, encouraging play and fun as well as cognitive and developmental growth.

The large, stately home where Josh lived couldn't have been more different. When Renee arrived, both his parents met us at the door. There was a two-story atrium in the entrance, and circular staircases wound up both sides of the large entryway. Josh was waiting at the top of the stairs. Low-volume classical music could be heard throughout the house, which was otherwise completely quiet. "We like it quiet," Josh's mom said. "When we get home from a hectic day, our house is our haven. We can go to our studies and recover. Even Josh has his own quiet study where he can go to read his little books."

No wonder Josh was having trouble with his first experience at school! (He had been mostly at home with a nanny until then). He was over-responsive to sensation to begin with, lacked auditory stimulation at home, and was overwhelmed by the "business" and noise of kindergarten. Among other things, OT recommendations included having Josh wear earphones at home to listen to children's music, starting at a very low volume and slowly increasing it over time. Action-oriented songs, to which Josh could move, would also help him integrate sound with more organizing proprioceptive and vestibular input. Music can be such an engaging experience for children and parents alike. Renee, the OT, took a minute to run to the car and grab one of the many CDs she had for her own young children to listen to while they were driving. They all pretended they were in a parade, and Josh's dad pretended he was beating a drum while Josh's mom held a pretend piccolo and tooted to the song playing on the CD. Everyone laughed together at how silly they all were being.

Josh, his parents, and his OT recognized that he sought deep pressure/tactile input when he was overwhelmed or dysregulated, especially in loud, crowded spaces. He liked to be held by his parents when they went to a store or other busy environment and would frequently ask for "bear hugs." His OT recognized that Josh already had some awareness of his sensory needs and told Josh that this was one of his superpowers! He was able to ask for what his body needed! They worked together to come up with some ways that they could decrease the overwhelming auditory input. Josh began wearing noise-canceling headphones in the classroom and in other overwhelming spaces (e.g., grocery store, school transitions, birthday parties). His parents adjusted their schedules (Culture) to run errands at less busy times so the stores were not as crowded (Environment). Josh liked wearing a weighted vest for short periods (up to 20 minutes) in these same environments, which helped his nervous system stay calm and organized. He didn't want to carry his favorite soft blanket in public (he was too big for that!) but his OT helped him cut a piece of the blanket to pin inside a pocket. This gave

Josh some more calming tactile input and something to focus on when spaces were too busy for him.

Jillian's Story

Eight-year-old Jillian has difficulty sitting and paying attention for any length of time. She is sensitive to a variety of sensations that she says make her feel like she wants to "run away and be alone." She typically doesn't have playdates, but today she has been invited to go to the movies with two other girls in her class. Her mother cringes, imagining how much of a struggle it might be for Jillian. Still, Jillian's mom goes back and forth between joy that her daughter has been invited and worry about how she might melt down at the movie theater.

In Jillian's case, the challenge is staying "tuned in" and not "melting down" in the movie theater. Her short attention span could be a potential social impediment and could affect whether she gets invited to hang out with friends again. Let's think about how we can use A SECRET to come up with strategies to engage Jillian's attention for the movie.

Problem-Solving: Using Sensation to support Jillian's success

Think about using *sensation* to help Jillian stay regulated so she will independently sit through the movie. Since Jillian has an over-responsive nervous system, sensation must be provided in a *low, slow* manner. Here are some strategies that Jillian's therapist suggested:

Weighted Items: Weight and pressure (both tactile inputs) have been found to be calming and organizing types of sensation for many sensitive children, and they can be helpful with any SPD subtype, not just over-responsivity. Most children become less reactive and less defensive when deep pressure sensory experiences are used just before or during the event, such as right before Jillian goes to the movie. The use of various weighted items like pressurized belts, socks, or vests (all of which may be found online—search the Web for "sensory therapy" and enter "heavy weight for treatment") may provide a calming effect on the nervous system (as with any other suggestion, it may not be the answer for every child). It's best to use this sensory input before the stimulating event to see how the child will respond. In Jillian's case, before she goes to the movies with her friends, but if it works for her, this strategy can be used unobtrusively during the event as well.

Proprioception or Heavy Work: Jillian's therapist can show her how to tie her sweatshirt sleeves around her shoulders and trunk and pull tightly to provide a hugging sensation. This exercise is loaded with deep pressure and proprioceptive input and may be helpful when the child is moving between classrooms or other school environments. In Jillian's case, this would be a useful method to use if she needs to leave her seat to use the bathroom or get a snack. Therapists often recommend brief proprioceptive exercises such as chair or wall push-ups, leg extensions with exercise band wrapped around chair legs, or delivering books to the library (not at the movies but in preparation).

Sensory Backpack: Jillian can bring her sensory backpack with her in the car on the way to the movies. Sensory backpacks are easily individualized with preferred sensory toys or tools for any child with challenges in any sensory domain or subtype. Jillian can use any of the comforting sensory objects in her backpack to help reduce anxiety or any sensory discomfort. The ultimate goal is for Jillian to self-regulate ahead of time in the car, knowing what she needs to do when she's beginning to feel overstimulated.

SAMPLE SENSORY BACKPACKS FOR SENSORY MODULATION DISORDERS

Sensory Over-Responsivity	Sensory Under-Responsivity	Sensory Craving
Familiar items	Jangling, oddly shaped items	Heavy objects or items with moving parts that are interesting and goal-related
Smooth items	Sticky and smellable items	Small hand weights, little gadget-like games
Soft, squishy items	"Pokey" items	Drawing-type games to keep kids busy with

Handheld computerized games |

Compression Jacket: At the movies, Jillian can use the compression-jacket trick, which is usually effective in providing calming input. This input will help keep Jillian from feeling bombarded by sensory input while sitting in close proximity to her friends in the theater.

Jillian may also want to buy some popcorn or candy to chew for oral motor stimulation during the movie. She can also drink from a sports water bottle with a nozzle or drink thick liquid (milkshake or smoothie) through a straw. These actions require sucking, which often provides calming proprioceptive input.

At age 8, Jillian desperately wants to have friends, but she and her mom are a little nervous about the upcoming movie date. She is worried that she won't be able to handle all the people, sounds, smells, and unexpected sensations that come up at the movies. Jillian and her parents and therapist can problem-solve ahead of time by openly talking about which sensations are most supportive for her, including her ideas in the conversation, and of course they can use other elements of A SECRET to support Jillian's success in this social situation!

Obviously, every child and every situation are different. There are a multitude of activities that you can use to help your child regulate before or after they feel over-aroused. Our goal is to show you how to use the problem-solving framework of A SECRET in a real-life situation. The strategies outlined here may have worked for Jillian, but they may not necessarily be useful for another child. *It's the thinking process that we're trying to convey here, not the specific activities!* You need to know how to think about and ask the right questions so you can figure out strategies that might be useful to your child at home or at school.

Sensation Strategies for Each Sensory System

The tables below provide strategies categorized by each sensory system. This is just one way to think about how to use *Sensation* to support your child's success. The table below lists strategies that are more calming and organizing. These *low-slow* sensations may be most useful with children who are over-responsive or dysregulated due to challenges with postural control, dyspraxia, or sensory discrimination.

CALMING AND ORGANIZING (LOW-SLOW) SENSATION STRATEGIES FOR CHILDREN NEEDING "LESS FUEL"

Sensory System	Strategies
Auditory	<ul><li>Use a soft voice and short sentences</li><li>Decrease the amount of language you use</li><li>Listen to soft music with lower frequencies</li><li>Play soft music, white noise, or relaxing environmental sounds</li><li>Wear earmuffs, or ear plugs</li><li>Offer noise-canceling headphones</li></ul>
Visual	<ul><li>Dim the lights</li><li>Use natural light and avoid fluorescent lighting</li><li>Leave the walls undecorated and use muted colors (soft blues, greens, tans)</li><li>Wear sunglasses or a baseball cap with a big brim</li></ul>

CALMING AND ORGANIZING (LOW-SLOW) SENSATION STRATEGIES FOR CHILDREN NEEDING "LESS FUEL"

Sensory System	Strategies
Gustatory (Taste)/Oral	• Suck on fruit or ice pops • Chew granola bars, fruit leather, or dried fruit • Implement incremental exposure—at mealtime, start with an empty plate and add only one food to it at a time • Warm drinks
Proprioceptive and Oral Proprioceptive	• Engage in isometric exercises, e.g., chair and wall push-ups • Work out with weights • Snack on chewy foods, chew gum, blow whistles or bubbles • Suck thick liquids through a straw • Drink from a sports water bottle with small nozzle • Have your child help with a proprioceptive task when you are away from home, like pushing a shopping cart, loading cans of food into the cart, and carrying the laundry • For deep pressure, wear pressure garments under the clothes, including Lycra and/or spandex garments. Also, give firm hugs and massages
Olfactory (Smell)	• Provide preferred aroma or fragrance to wear, like lavender, vanilla, or cinnamon

CALMING AND ORGANIZING (LOW-SLOW) SENSATION STRATEGIES FOR CHILDREN NEEDING "LESS FUEL"

Sensory System	Strategies
Tactile	• Use weighted objects, like weighted lap pillows, weighted blankets, and weighted stuffed animals • Roll and/or wrap the child in blankets and warm towels. For sleeping, use cotton quilts and smooth sleeping bags. Place pieces of soft fabric on pillowcases and use flannel sheets • Take a warm bath • Provide extra toweling-off after a bath • Offer fidget toys, Koosh balls, silly putty, and bendable figures
Vestibular (Movement)	• Have the child swing on a swing-set in a slow, linear motion • Rock or glide in a chair with the child sitting in your lap
Interoceptive (Internal Sensations)	• Use a hot water bottle for stomachaches • Take a warm bath • Eat soup and drink decaffeinated herbal teas, either hot or cold • Apply ice to new bruises

The *fast-blast* strategies listed in this table are more alerting. These strategies should be used with children who are under-responsive, crave sensation, or have difficulty staying alert and attentive; these are children who often need "more fuel."

ALERTING (FAST-BLAST) SENSATION STRATEGIES FOR CHILDREN NEEDING "MORE FUEL"

Sensory System	Strategies
Auditory	• Play music with a fast or irregular beat • Try unexpected sounds or background noise during homework • Set a clock or phone alarm to indicate time for a sensory break
Visual	• Bright lights • Alerting colors (red, orange, yellow) and wall decorations • High contrast colors for worksheets (e.g., black text on yellow paper) • Busy classroom setting
Gustatory (Taste)/Oral	• Spicy foods • Crunchy vegetables • Crunchy foods • Cold liquids • Ice chips
Proprioceptive	• Play games that include irregular, fast movements with frequent stop and go (e.g., tag, chase, races with obstacles) • Tug-of-war • Jumping on a trampoline

ALERTING (FAST-BLAST) SENSATION STRATEGIES FOR CHILDREN NEEDING "MORE FUEL"

Sensory System	Strategies
Olfactory	• Cinnamon • Sour or bitter smells • Strong odors
Tactile	• Light unexpected touch • Varied textures • Mixed food textures • Tickling games (Be careful with this! Tickling can be very overwhelming)
Vestibular	• Stop/go games • Dancing • Jump and crash activities
Interoceptive (Internal Sensations)	• Play with toys in cold water • Use exaggerated affect (facial gestures and sounds) to call attention to internal signals

Common Organizing Sensation Activities for Any SPD Subtype

Self-Directed Tactile Stimulation

Children with sensory over-responsivity do not want others to impose tactile input on them. They may, however, tolerate and even seek out tactile activities in which they are in control of the intensity and duration of the stimuli. Encourage touch input by offering a wide variety of possible tactile materials, such as brushes and vibrating toys.

Provide Comforting Sensory Input

No child should ever be forced to endure tactile stimulation that feels uncomfortable. We strongly recommend against "pushing the child through it" to make a neurological change related to tactile defensiveness. Do the means justify the end? No; it just isn't worth it. We do not want to add to the child's traumatic memories of touch. When a child becomes ready for various levels of tactile input, you'll be able to tell. We recommend that parents shop at inexpensive stores for paintbrushes, bath brushes, and other tactile materials that feel *good* to the child. A large fabric shop is a great place to find out what materials feel good. It is simple to let your child choose "special" material for a pillowcase, which can be made by sewing two simple seams in one piece of cloth.

Oral Sensation

Depending on temperature and consistency, food can affect arousal and help provide organizing input to your child. Cold food and drinks have more of an arousing effect, and warm foods can be calming. Try ice pops or ice chips, hard candies, crunchy foods, or gum to increase arousal and attention. Warm, sweet, and chewy foods generally have calming effects. Sour, salty, bitter, and spicy flavors may be alerting for a child who is under-responsive or who likes a lot of sensory input.

Sucking is like a "heavy-work" activity for the mouth. Sometimes sucking thick foods like applesauce, yogurt, or pudding can be extremely calming for a child with sensory over-responsivity.

Incorporate Calming Stimulation into Daily Life
Activities and Routines

One example of calming stimulation is incorporating calming games into bath time. For example, taking a deep breath and blowing bubbles or soap suds, or plunging floating toys under the water. The warm water itself can be very calming, along with essential oil (such as lavender) or other preferred scents.

Heavy Work

The following list of activities can be used to enhance relationships between peers and families while helping a child benefit from the organized sensation of tactile input and proprioception. These activities can be done with the child to enhance the "readiness state" (*a*) prior to doing a task that may be difficult, (*b*) between each individual step of a challenging task, or (*c*) following a difficult task. The activities described here use heavy work to provide a calming influence on a child who may be dysregulated.

- *Sand Play:* Shoveling and playing in the sand engages muscles and joints (heavy work), especially if the sand is wet!

- *Gardening:* Another excellent activity is gardening. Digging, moving dirt, repotting soil, carrying gardening tools, and helping transplant plants all make good use of muscles and joints and provide great proprioceptive input to calm children who tend to get overresponsive quickly. This would be a great activity for children before an overstimulating event such as going to dinner with extended family.

- **Water Play:** Most kids love to play in water, and water is actually quite heavy. The larger the sponge, the heavier it is. The bigger the bucket, the heavier it is. Using a little ingenuity, it can be easy to devise a "chore" that's both fun and therapeutic! Washing the car would be a wonderful activity to do right before an event that you know will be over-stimulating, such as a birthday party.

- **Chores:** Many chores require "heavy work," and children may do them just to help you out. Examples include carrying laundry or groceries, returning books to the school library, making the bed, and stacking chairs in the classroom. Keep in mind that your purpose is to calm down a child whose arousal is high. What other household tasks might help lower your child's overall arousal level?

Reflection

Which sensory systems seem to be supportive for your child (what types of sensation do they prefer or go to when they are upset)? Touch? Deep pressure? Heavy work? Sounds? Low lights?

_____

_____

_____

_____

_____

_____

_____

_____

_____

What sensations are most challenging for your child?

_____

_____

_____

_____

_____

_____

_____

_____

6: SENSATION

What activities or environments can you identify as being especially challenging for your child?

_____

_____

_____

_____

_____

_____

_____

_____

How do you build sensation into your family culture?

_____

_____

_____

_____

_____

_____

_____

_____

_____

How can you include your child think up new ideas for touch sensation?

_____

_____

_____

_____

_____

_____

_____

_____

Below, we provide some examples of *Sensation* strategies, or what we call process points. These examples will not fit every child or family but should be used as a guide. The reflection above should help you think about your personal culture and your family or classroom culture. Use the reflection to think about *Sensation* process points that will work for you.

A SECRET

Challenge Area	Attunement	Sensation	Emotion Regulation	Culture	Relationship	Environment	Task
	⟳	• Work with your child to help them recognize their sensory strengths & challenges	⟳				
	⟳	• Recognize & call attention to your own sensory needs & differences					
		• Have sensory tools easily available at home & school		⟳			
		• Teach your child to use sensory tools independently					⟳
		• Create a sensory corner with your child. Consider including items that provide calming touch, deep pressure, favorite music, or cozy seating			⟳	⟳	
		• Help your child fill a sensory backpack with calming tools (fidget toys, weighted animals, scented bean bag up to 10% of body weight, etc.)	⟳				
		• Create a culture of *Sensation* for your sensory craver (frequent sensory breaks during the day, family walk after dinner, dance parties, stand-up desk for homework, daily chores, etc.)		⟳	⟳		⟳

CHAPTER 7

EMOTION REGULATION

E = Emotion Regulation

What is Emotional Regulation?

A SECRET							
Challenge Area	Attunement	Sensation	Emotion Regulation	Culture	Relation-ship	Environment	Task

Emotion regulation is a complex construct with different definitions depending on the audience or the professional discipline. Some claim that emotion regulation is synonymous with emotional control (Zimmer-Gembeck & Skinner, 2016). Therefore, we have to be able to monitor and evaluate our emotional experiences to have a regulated response to emotions. This requires awareness and discrimination of a range of physiological responses to emotion (being aware and paying attention to how our bodies react to emotion). This is what we call a top-down process, one that requires higher-level brain functioning, or the ability to *evaluate and respond*, as discussed in chapter 2. This ability to acknowledge and discriminate emotions does not even begin in typical develop until later in childhood, even adolescence (Compas et al., 2017). It is important to understand that awareness and discrimination of emotions is a significant challenge for most of our kids with SPD.

Others define emotion regulation as more of an automatic function that occurs at lower (subcortical) levels of the brain. As mentioned in chapter 2, this is what we call the *Regulate* function. By this definition, emotion regulation is an involuntary process that occurs in response to one's environment (Compas, Connor-Smith, & Jaser, 2004), including, of course, sensory information in our immediate surroundings. What is clear from the literature is that it is essential to characterize or define your own working definition of emotion regulation.

For the purposes of this book, we define *Emotion Regulation* as the lower-level brain ability to Regulate responses to emotion. Using this definition, we consider a child's ability to respond to "big" emotions (positive or negative) by observing related behaviors. In this chapter, we provide strategies to build lower-level *Emotion Regulation* or self-regulation strategies, and also more "top-down" or cognitive strategies to help children (and caregivers) use higher-level coping strategies. Another way to think about the meaning of emotional regulation is to consider how complicated it is to control *your own* emotions. Think about the last really close call you had in a car because someone didn't watch where they were going. You probably had an instantaneous emotional response composed of three factors:

1. Your feelings (e.g., anger or fear)
2. Your instantaneous thoughts related to the situation (e.g., "This is just like last time when I was in an accident")
3. Unconscious physiological reactions to what happened (e.g., your heart starts pumping faster)

We all respond to the combination of these factors. Our kids' responses include acting out, throwing temper tantrums, screaming, hitting, and exhibiting other "bad" behaviors.

Regulating your own emotional responses is critical to getting along in life. Usually when something bothers you, you can just let it go unless it's really important. You don't blurt out every little thought about it, because you've learned to control what stays inside your head versus what you say out loud (at least most of the time).

This chapter uses examples and strategies that can apply to children of any subtype who demonstrate difficulties with regulating their emotions. A lack of control in this area is the most common reason children with SPD are referred to occupational therapy. Research has shown that social skills and emotional regulation are two of the most important characteristics needed for success in school (Lewit & Baker, 1995). In addition, emotional regulation is an even better predictor of school readiness than Intelligence Quotient (IQ) scores from standardized testing (Blair & Razza, 2007). Interestingly, attention regulation has been shown to correlate with measures of school readiness (Johnson et al., 2003) Even at the preschool age, regulation predicts later academic competence (Blair & Razza, 2007) and portends both verbal and quantitative SAT Test scores many years later (Shoda, Mischel, & Peake, 1990).

For example, Jose is a youngster with a 'quick trigger' responding in ways at times that are difficult for his teacher. One day, Jose is playing Jenga with his friend Tommy and seems excited and happy. The next day he plays Jenga again but appears angry and frustrated with everyone and everything. The longer he tries to play the more frustrated he gets, and the bigger his outbursts become. It seems to him that every time he moves a block, the tower falls. He is desperately unhappy and becomes aggressive. Jose says, "I hate this game. It is so unfair. I hate you, Tommy, I am never going to play with you ever again!"

We can use the analogy of a cup to think about Jose's capacity for emotion regulation. Stressors or big emotions may fill a cup to the point of overflowing, and that's usually when a meltdown will occur. A cup that is half-full has room to take in more emotions, sensory information, or other types of stressors. When we use strategies to support emotion regulation, we are able to release some stress and stop our cups from overflowing. Figure 7.1 shows a cup filling up with emotions, sensory input, and other challenges, but also has the capacity to release some of that built-up stress to avoid a meltdown. When we use Emotion Regulation strategies to support success in our kids, we are keeping their cups from overflowing and teaching them that they have some control to support their own emotion regulation.

Figure 7.1 The Emotion Regulation cup

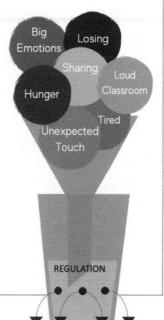

Of course, this is a simplistic explanation. In reality, life is rarely so black and white. But if you understand and keep the arousal curve in mind, you will discover amazing things about another person's emotional readiness to win or lose in that moment and on that day. And you can base your actions on that knowledge.

Jose's teacher is confused by his behavior because it seems inconsistent and hard to predict. But if you step back and observe Jose's behaviors, it is clear he is having difficulty regulating his emotions. On the first day, he has room in his emotion regulation cup for both wins and losses. But on the second day, Jose's cup is almost full when he starts playing, and one little loss puts him over his quotient, so he snaps (it's like the straw that broke the camel's back). This is why it's essential to be attuned or to try to read both boy's emotional state before starting the game.

Being aware of Jose's sensory differences will allow the teacher to understand his support needs and his stressors. She may be able to make some changes to the *Environment* by having the boys play in a quiet, uncluttered corner of the room. It may also be helpful to provide preferred sensory input to help Jose organize his nervous system (*Sensation*, like sitting on partially inflated seat cushion or doing 10 chair push-ups before playing). To support the development of *Emotion Regulation*, it may be helpful to use a top-down strategy with the entire class. There are many tools available now to help build awareness of arousal regulation or changes in emotional state. Some examples include The Zones of Regulation® (Kuypers, 2011) The Alert Program®, Williams & Shellenberger, 1996) or The Incredible 5-point Scale (Buron & Curtis, 2003). All children at this age benefit from improving self-regulation skills, and this way Jose isn't singled out!

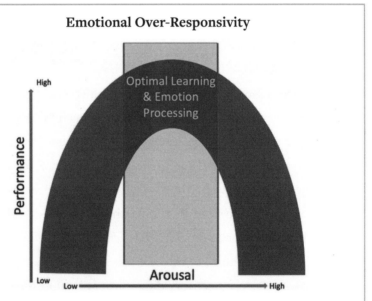

Figure 7.2 The arousal curve is an over-simplification of arousal regulation (Yerkes-Dodson Law), but it can be a helpful way to understand why our children jump quickly to over-arousal or dysregulation.

Steven's Story

Steven, a five-year-old kindergarten student who loves science and recess, engages well during circle time and is generally kind to his teachers and classmates. However, Steven has a difficult time with transitions during center time. Steven loves the center with the rice table and enjoys finding hidden objects inside the tactile sensorium. He frequently tantrums and becomes aggressive toward his peers when asked to move from this center.

Miss Elvira, the classroom teacher, says, "Okay, class, we have three more minutes before we have to switch centers. Remember, when I clap my hands together, we will need to move to the next center."

"No way, I am staying here. This is my rice table, and I am not going to move! I hate the handwriting and math centers!" Steven says.

Miss Elvira claps her hands, and the students begin to rotate to the other centers.

"Move, Steven, your turn is over, move away now! Miss Elvira clapped her hands," another student shouts.

"No! My turn is not over! I am not moving!" Steven shouts back as he begins to push the other students away.

"Stop pushing me, Steven. You are hurting me," says Emily, a sweet classmate who is always compliant and shares with Steven.

"I didn't mean to hurt you, Emily, but I am not moving!" Steven shouts.

At this point, there is chaos in the class and all the students are crying and yelling at Steven for being unfair and aggressive. Steven is having a temper tantrum, throwing himself on the floor, and refusing to rotate to any other center.

Miss Elvira calmly walks over to the other students and says, "Okay, that's it, everyone. No more rice table, we are done with centers! Please return to your seats."

Steven continues crying and kicking his feet. The other students are scared and remain motionless. The teacher is conflicted about Steven's behavior and does not know what to do as the class falls more and more into disarray. She does not understand why Steven acts this way and why he is so obsessed with the rice table.

Because the other students are upset and appear to be almost frozen while Steven is still screaming, Miss Elvira makes a decision to take the class out to the playground to cool down before asking them to do more work. Miss Elvira realizes that the class is in shutdown mode, as is Steven (*Attunement*). She understands that Steven is struggling with emotion regulation and that the best thing to do for the class is to change the environment, so she moves them from the classroom to a place that all the students enjoy. She is conflicted as she realizes the importance of tactile play and sensory motor skill development that the rice center offers to the class. She does not want to remove the table from the centers.

Miss Elvira asks Agnes, the OT, to meet with her to discuss Stephen and the way she ran the class. Agnes heard about the issues occurring in class during center time. She asks Miss Elvira if the class has a visual schedule that shows all the activities and events that will occur during the day.

Agnes suggests, "Steven may need his own visual schedule on his desk or on a clipboard that clearly shows him the different events for the day. We can make little pictures of all the centers and activities that he will be involved in and put Velcro strips on the chart so when he completes an activity, he gets to put it into the completed envelope. I won't be able to make thorough recommendations until I do an evaluation, but you can submit a referral to our team for an assessment."

At the end of the evaluation, Agnes writes impact statements to describe the impact of sensory processing challenges on participation and success in school environment. She highlights Steven's individual sensory differences and how they may be impacting his ability to participate in schoolwork or peer interactions.

The Impact of Poor Sensory Modulation on Self-Regulation and Social Interactions

Sensory modulation is the ability to take in sensory input while regulating the degree, intensity, or frequency of response to the input. Given accurate modulation of sensations, children can accurately grade their responses to different and unexpected sensations, while maintaining an optimal level of arousal. Poor sensory modulation is impacting Steven's arousal level and thus his ability to transition from activities that make him feel comfortable and in control.

Steven's sensory modulation challenges are varied. He demonstrates over-responsivity to some sensations, such as unexpected light touch and sound. Sensory craving behaviors include constantly seeking soft textures, deep pressure, and movement (e.g., jumping and crashing). Because of his sensory modulation challenges, Steven is easily dysregulated throughout the day, which explains his exaggerated reactions to seemingly small challenges. In this "fight or flight" state, Steven has difficulty accepting limits and following directions, and often cannot respond to attempts to help him regulate. This is also why he cannot use words in the moment to explain how he's feeling or why he is upset. When the body is at this heightened state of arousal, the brain is not functioning optimally. Far from being able to reason or process emotions (*Evaluate and Respond*), Steven's brain is functioning at the Protect and React level and just trying to regulate.

Agnes provides the written evaluation report to Miss Elvira and adds:

> "I have ideas for other strategies that might help, and I can come into your classroom and try them out. For example, it might be helpful if we add a timed timer to give a visual representation of the amount of time left before the next transition. Steven seems very sensitive to sound, and I think the visuals may work better for him than clapping, especially when he is in an agitated state." (*Sensation*).

Miss Elvira understands that there is more to this situation than she is able to assess in her busy classroom. She and Agnes work together, discussing the findings from the Sensory Profile School Companion (Dunn, 2006) and Agnes' observations in various school settings, including center time, the lunchroom, recess, and the transition to art class. They identify Steven's sensory differences and discuss strategies to help him stay regulated in the classroom.

Miss Elvira also works with the entire class to build emotion regulation capacities with all of the children. She has a big traffic light picture posted on the wall, and children place their name on the traffic light to show how they're feeling (red is fast/frustrated/upset/anxious/ etc., yellow is getting anxious/feeling worried/confused; green is calm/ regulated/happy/just right). When she recognizes that the whole class is in the yellow light, Miss Elvira will have all the students stop and take 10 deep breaths, do two yoga poses, or identify five green things in the classroom. These strategies help the whole class calm down and return to the green zone.

Resources for Emotion Regulation

Many Emotion Regulation tools are available for kids these days. Here are a few resources:

Yoga Calm: *yogacalm.org*

Yoga Pretzels: *yogaed.com/store/yoga-pretzel-deck*

Mindful Kids: *altiplano.com*

Incredible 5 Point Scale: *www.5pointscale.com*

Steven loves the rice table because of the soothing tactile input that he experiences when he is at that center. His tantrums are a result of his challenges with incoming sensation and how quickly he becomes overloaded when pulled away from this preferred sensory input. The rice table can be a predictable, self-controlled, sensory grounding experience for Steven.

Steven likes to interact with Emily. She is always nice to him and is a sweet, quiet, little girl. Though Steven is motivated to play with Emily, he often becomes frustrated during play because his sensory modulation challenges cause him to become easily over-aroused. He will play with her for a short time at the sand table but ultimately reverts back to solitary, self-absorbed play, with Emily on the sideline. He is overwhelmed by the number of students in the classroom and becomes irritated and overwhelmed when he has to sit at other centers in close proximity to his peers. He acts out in music class but does well in his art class, where he actively engages in tactile and proprioceptive activities involving playdough, stamping, finger painting, etc.

Agnes plans to provide 'push in' services for Steven (working in the classroom instead of pulling him out for one-on-one therapy). When Agnes comes into the classroom to see Steven, she can work on expanding activities to add more heavy work. In addition, she can determine how Steven might join play with a small group of children. Then she can share these ideas with Miss Elvira. When Agnes gets into the classroom, she says to Steven:

"Steven, I have a special little fidget that you can keep in your pocket.

It is a squishy gel ball with little stars inside that show up when you squeeze it. Would you like to play with it while we're here in the classroom? Some kids find it helps them to stay calm."

Steven says, "Yes, I would like that! I will have it with me whenever I am here, starting today." He shows Agnes how he squeezes the ball, with a big smile on his face. He is obviously happy and feeling listened to, understood, and accepted (*Relationship*).

At the next team meeting, Agnes consults with the teacher and psychologist to discuss her concern for Steven's social challenges at school. The teacher and psychologist agree that a small support group, such as a lunch bunch, might be helpful for Steven.

Agnes says:

"I notice that Steven gravitates to Emily. She is always trying to play with Steven and is very willing to share toys with him. Could we move Steven to the side of the classroom, maybe toward the back, away from the windows and doors, so there are fewer distractions? Could Emily have her desk placed near Steven's so they can work as a buddy team? I think if he starts off with a student who is kind to him, his behavior might improve."

The psychologist and teacher agree, and Miss Elvira says, "Great idea! I will move the desks into pairs and create buddy systems for everyone (*Culture*). Steven does like Emily and seeks her out in class. He is always sad when she cries or if he thinks he has hurt or upset her. This will help him solidify this classroom relationship."

Discussion of Vignette: Emotion Regulation

This scene looks at many aspects of how A SECRET can be used in the classroom. Many factors are introduced into this story, including the teacher's attunement and empathy toward Steven. Her communication and collaboration with Agnes and the psychologist show a collaborative team effort, which allows for a clearer understanding of what drives Steven's behavior and how they might support him to be more successful in the classroom.

The addition of the visual time timer, visual schedule, and the fidget are great contributions to support success, but the pairing of the desks to facilitate a peer relationship is an essential cultural shift ⟳. Steven responded well to these new changes, and Emily fit nicely into the role of his companion in class. The class centers became less chaotic, as the whole class benefited from reminders provided by the Time Timer.

This story provides a small snapshot of Steven throughout the day. Let's see if we can use the A SECRET chart to look at how the team helped Steven transition from one center to the next.

Strategies for Emotional Regulation

It is essential to understand that emotion regulation is a complex developmental process. For our children with SPD, it often develops much later than in neurotypical children. One of the most important things we can do is try to understand the process of emotion regulation development and the additional challenges brought on by SPD. As is true with the other elements of A SECRET, the strategies laid out in this chapter will need to be adapted for each child. It is easy to expect that our children understand the physical sensations that they are experiencing and that they can relate those sensations to emotions. However, that is usually not the case. So, one of the first steps in the process is to help children connect to their bodies or to their basic senses: touch, sight, sound, smell, and taste. Your occupational therapist, counselor, psychologist, or other mental health provider will be essential resources for helping you adjust your expectations and meet your child where they are in the emotion regulation process.

This first set of strategies may be useful for children who have poor bodily and emotional awareness. This is often the case with children who are under-responsive or who have poor discrimination or sensory-based motor challenges. Before we use words or cognitive strategies to identify emotions, we need to help them connect to their bodies, so basic sensory awareness is a better place to start.

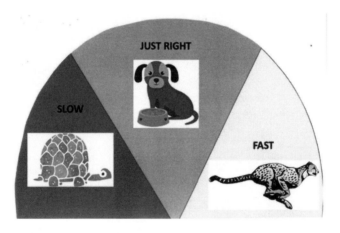

Figure 7.3 We use this scale to help young children attend to changes in their arousal levels during play. If children are interested, they can help you pick out pictures to represent *slow*, *just right*, and *fast*.

For children who are more aware of their bodies and their physical responses to emotion, you can begin to use cognitive strategies to support further development of emotion regulation. Simple but targeted activities can be used for this purpose.

Play games that involve the whole body and refer to changes in arousal or physical state. It is usually helpful to have a visual. We use the Engine Scale (adapted from Williams & Shellenberger 1996; see Figure 7.4) to help children recognize shifts in their arousal and they are playing. For example: "Wow, this game is making me feel fun fast! I'm laughing and starting to sweat! I think I need to slow my body down a little bit."

Figure 7.4 Use the Engine Scale (adapted from Williams & Shellenberger, 1996) to help children connect to physical sensations in their bodies when they are moving and playing.

Describe your own feelings or emotional states. This is a great way to call attention to emotions for children who are just becoming aware. Point out and label your emotions and the physical responses you are feeling. For example: "I'm noticing that my heart is beating faster, and I have a tight feeling in my stomach. I'm going to take a break because I'm feeling too fast."

Be attuned to your child's emotions. Make educated guesses about your child's emotional state. "I see that you've stopped smiling and laughing. It looks like you are feeling sad." Ask your child to tell you if you are "right" or "wrong." Reinforce how important it is to learn to interpret cues in faces, body language, and the manner in which words are said. This strategy will work with some children, but for others it can be dysregulating to even call attention to their emotions. Be attuned to your child's process, and don't push if they aren't ready for this!

One project you can do together is to cut out pictures from magazines or old family photos that you can talk about together. Point out how facial expressions relate to specific feelings. Have your child look at a picture of themselves. Maybe these photos trigger feelings of glee and happiness or sadness and fear. See if your child can show you how they were feeling when that photograph was taken. This type of activity can help the child recapture that emotional state and apply it to future situations.

For children who are in the early stages of developing emotion regulation, it may be difficult to recognize and pay attention to emotions, especially for our children with SPD to help them connect to body signals, so looking at pictures or playing emotion-based board games may not help them recognize internal states. This is why we like to start with using the engine scale and paying attention to body signals and changes in arousal level. When kids are moving and playing, it can be much easier to recognize internal signals.

Use pretend play to practice emotional regulation strategies. Following your child's lead in play can provide opportunities to play out scary or frustrating feelings. Let them lead these play themes and be in charge. Being there to support, organize, and join in the play is important. You are listening to their stories, acknowledging their emotions, and helping them feel safe.

You may also think about introducing games that subtly and playfully challenge your child (but be careful! Follow their lead and DON'T push if they aren't ready). For example, play a game in which your child pretends they love "yucky" foods (and make sure they know they don't have to eat it). This is a cognitive behavioral approach that helps teach children how to remain controlled when faced with negative stimuli. Both behavioral and subjective signs of negative emotions can change with this cognitive approach.

Develop strategies to build emotional regulation. Every teacher likely has at least one child in a classroom who has challenges with emotional regulation. It's important to remember that emotion regulation is a developmental capacity. Neurotypical children also benefit from strategies to support social-emotional development! To facilitate learning for all students in the class, children must trust their teacher and know that the environment will stay safe and fairly predictable. One method that can reinforce a safe, predictable classroom environment is to have the class set a few rules—typically fewer than eight—during the first week of school. For example, keep hands and feet to yourself, stay on your carpet square at circle time, line up on numbers on the floor (visual cue) and wait for the teacher's signal, and raise your hand if you want to speak. It may be helpful to review the rules weekly. This structure helps create a sense of safety and predictability in the classroom.

If the rules are violated, use a natural consequence or a disciplinary action related to the violation. For example, if a student writes on their desk, they can clean the tops of all the desks. For more disruptive situations, teachers may find time away from the hectic classroom helpful. Instead of calling this a "timeout," create a space where the child can have a sensory break. It may help the child regulate if they can go to another room to calm down for 15 to 20 minutes.

Understand your own emotional regulation strategies. We all have strategies to help us deal with stress. Understanding what works for you can be a tremendous leap toward helping children with poor emotional regulation. Try to verbalize what strategies you use and see whether they may be helpful to children with emotional regulation difficulties.

Reconnect or "repair" with your child after a meltdown or disagreement. It isn't possible to stay calm, cool, and collected all the time, especially during meltdowns. It's okay to lose your cool (and even yell) sometimes, but it's the "repair" that's important. Take time to reconnect with your child after a disconnect. (*Relationship*; see chapter 10 for more information)

Practice emotional regulation activities with your child. See if you can interest your child in activities that will help them learn methods of self-regulation. For example, find a parent-child yoga or Taekwondo class. Mindfulness is a great tool for building emotion regulation by teaching awareness of sensations, emotions, and thoughts. It's a way of helping your child focus and attend to one physical sensation (e.g., breathing), sound, or mental image to help diffuse overwhelming feelings.

Build sensory awareness—early mindfulness. Play a game with sensation. Have your child close their eyes and pay attention to one sense at a time, then have them name everything they can hear (or feel, touch, smell) in 30 seconds. For younger children you may need to start with 5 or 10 seconds at a time and build up from there.

Reflection

How does your child respond to big emotions, even positive ones?

_____

_____

_____

_____

_____

_____

_____

_____

_____

Is your child aware of changes in arousal (when their body is feeling fast or slow)? Can they pay attention with senses? How can you build these skills into daily routines or your family Culture?

_____

_____

_____

_____

_____

_____

_____

_____

Consider your child's ability to "use their words" to describe emotions. Perhaps they need to build awareness of sensations or arousal changes before they're ready for emotion awareness. What tools or strategies might you use to help them build this developmental capacity?

_____

_____

_____

_____

_____

_____

_____

What tools do you use to keep yourself calm when your child is melting down? How do you and your child "repair" after a meltdown or argument?

_____

_____

_____

7: EMOTION REGULATION

_____

_____

_____

_____

_____

_____

References

Cai, R. Y., Richdale, A. L., Uljarević, M., Dissanayake, C., & Samson, A. C. (2018). Emotion regulation in autism spectrum disorder: Where we are and where we need to go. *Autism Research, 11*(7), 962-978.

Cole, P. M., Armstrong, L. M., & Pemberton, C. K. (2010). The role of language in the development of emotion regulation. In S. D. Calkins & M. A. Bell (Eds.), Human brain development. *Child Development at the Intersection of Emotion and Cognition* (p. 59–77). American Psychological Association. https://doi.org/10.1037/12059-004

Compas, B.E., Connor-Smith, J.K., & Jaser, S.S. (2004). Temperament, stress reactivity, and coping: Implications for depression in childhood and adolescence. *Journal of Clinical Child and Adolescent Psychology, 33*, 21–31. https://doi:10.1207/S15374424JCCP3301_3

Blair, C., & Razza, R. P. (2007). Relating effortful control, executive function, and false belief understanding to emerging math and literacy ability in kindergarten. *Child Development, 78*(2), 647-663.

Buron, K. D., & Curtis, M. (2003). *The incredible 5-point scale: Assisting students with autism spectrum disorders in understanding social interactions and controlling their emotional responses.* AAPC Publishing.

Dunn, W. (2006). *Sensory Profile School Companion: User's Manual.* San Antonio, TX: Psychological Corporation.

Johnson, D. J., Jaeger, E., Randolph, S. M., Cauce, A. M., Ward, J., & National Institute of Child Health and Human Development Early Child Care Research Network. (2003). Studying the effects of early child care experiences on the development of children of color in the United States: Toward a more inclusive research agenda. *Child Development*, 74(5), 1227-1244.

Kuypers, L. (2011). *The Zones of Regulation*. San Jose: Think Social Publishing.

Lewit, E.M, Baker LS. School readiness. *Future Child*. 1995; 5(2):128-139.

Martin, R. E., & Ochsner, K. N. (2016). The neuroscience of emotion regulation development: Implications for education. *Current Opinion in Behavioral Sciences*, 10, 142-148.

Shoda, Y., Mischel, W., & Peake, P. K. (1990). Predicting adolescent cognitive and self-regulatory competencies from preschool delay of gratification: Identifying diagnostic conditions. *Developmental psychology*, 26(6), 978.

Williams, M. S., & Shellenberger, S. (1996). *How does your engine run?: A leader's guide to the alert program for self-regulation*. TherapyWorks, Inc.

Zimmer-Gembeck MJ, & Skinner, E.A. (2016). The development of coping: Implications for psychopathology and resilience In Cicchetti D (Ed.), *Developmental Psychopathology*. Oxford, England: Wiley & Sons.

On the next page, we provide some examples of *Emotion Regulation* strategies, or what we call process points. These examples will not fit every child or family but should be used as a guide. The reflection above should help you think about supports and challenges in this element of A SECRET. Use the reflection to think about *Emotion Regulation* process points that will work for your family or your child's classroom.

A SECRET

Challenge Area	Attunement	Sensation	Emotion Regulation	Culture	Relationship	Environment	Task
	⟳		• Use a visual to help your child become aware of changes in their arousal regulation				
	⟳		• Model your own emotion awareness. Use visuals to call attention to your arousal changes and moments when you need to slow down or take a break				
		⟳	• Schedule regular one-on-one play sessions with your child (even if it's only 5 minutes a day). Set a timer and let them know that this is your special time. Follow their lead and let them be in control of the play	⟳	⟳		

			• Provide routine and structure during transitions or in new environments
			  – Use a sensory backpack for transitions
			  – Create a visual schedule with photos of what comes next
				⟳	⟳		⟳

			• Create a safe or quiet space for calming down
			  – Plan this space with your child
			  – Include a cozy pillow or blanket
			  – Fill a box or basket of preferred sensory tools
			  – Let your child know that this space is NOT a punishment or timeout
					⟳	⟳ ⟳	

CHAPTER 8

CULTURE

C = Culture

How do we use Culture to support success?

A SECRET							
Challenge Area	Attunement	Sensation	Emotion Regulation	Culture	Relation-ship	Environment	Task

In the first edition of *No Longer A Secret*, we defined culture as the way things are usually done regarding customs, context, habits, or conditions creating a way of life that generates the atmosphere or *culture* of your family or classroom. We also used it interchangeably with *context* or *current conditions*. In this chapter, we attempt to clearly define what we mean by the construct of *Culture*. Because this is an essential component of A SECRET (as we believe all of them are!) we will be consistent with our terminology and stick with the term "culture." For example, at school, *Culture* includes eating lunch then going out for recess and having "specials" like art or music in the afternoon. For young children, starting the day with circle time is part of the classroom *Culture*.

Culture, by our definition, does not refer solely to ethnic, regional, or biological background. Yes, we are referring to customs, habits, or routines, perhaps within a family or a classroom. We are also looking deeper into the connections between a child and caregiver, and among families. *Culture* is a construct that is individual, dynamic, and relational (Bonder, Martine, and Miracle, 2004). *Culture*, or patterns of behavior, develop from the interactions between individuals or among groups, so each person creates their own unique culture and adapts to fit certain group norms or expectations. As therapists, we work closely with the child and family or teacher to understand patterns of behavior and preferences. We observe children's interactions with family members and peers and in different settings (home, classroom, community, etc.). This can help us create interventions and home programs that consider individual values, preferences for activities (*Task*), types of interaction (*Relationship*), and, of course, sensory differences (*Sensation*) ! The more we take the time to observe and understand individual cultural differences, the better we will be at problem-solving creative strategies to create a sensory lifestyle.

Desmond's Story

For some students, riding home on the school bus, having a quick snack, and then rushing off to soccer practice is part of their family *Culture*. In this example, if a child is struggling with soccer, there are many of ways of changing the *Culture* to make them more successful.

Desmond felt defeated even before the start of each soccer game. His mom, Viola, decided she would change the *Culture* to make it more positive and to support his self-esteem. She decided to try picking him up from school rather than having him take the bus home. She brought a few snacks so he could choose what he wanted, giving him a little control. Finally, they decided together to make the drive a fun Mom-and-Desmond time (*Relationship*) . Each time Viola picked Desmond up for practice, they would pick a song to sing together during the drive. Having this fun time together helped Desmond transition to soccer practice feeling "just right" and more ready to participate. Viola also spoke to Desmond about participating in other sports. Viola gave him the choice to offer him more control, and he decided to stay on the soccer team to be with his friends. Desmond and Viola worked together to create a few changes in their culture and came up with a plan that was more supportive for him and fit with the whole family.

We can also look at cultural shifts in the public and private school sectors. Many districts now offer inclusive classrooms for students who may have struggled in traditional classroom settings. Inclusion refers to general education classrooms where students with and without learning differences or other special education needs work and learn together. To help students meet academic goals, activities and subject matter are adapted to support individual learning needs. Many students with sensory and motor challenges may benefit from learning in an inclusive setting, and the school OT can help with adaptations and modifications.

In this way, classrooms can be equipped with the necessary tools and the educational framework to promote inclusive spaces where students with special needs can learn. The one-size-fits-all notion that is common in some general education classrooms may require a cultural shift to support more diverse learners.

Within the inclusive school setting, students with an Individualized Education Plan receive ancillary services. Often, the therapist helps the teacher and teaching assistant problem-solve what to modify to fit the child. Suggestions and recommendations made by the occupational therapist often require a change in classroom routines or culture. Creating these cultural changes in the classroom can be tricky and requires an open mind and flexibility from all. It is important to note how all the elements within A SECRET can be impacted and influenced by altering one element .

Cultural Shifts Due to COVID-19

The outbreak of COVID-19 facilitated many unexpected cultural changes within the school setting. Teachers and school administrators rushed to meet recommended safety guidelines that were necessary for students to access education and socialization in a safe environment. A SECRET may be helpful in problem-solving new ways to support student success in this altered classroom culture. Here are just a few of the cultural changes that occurred during the coronavirus outbreak:

- Required mask-wearing
- Physical distancing—spacing desks sit 6 feet apart
- Plexiglass barriers, which allow for socialization but impact peer relationships
- Staggered schedules
- Online learning
- Regular temperature and health checks

So, you're ready to start observing individual and group culture! You're looking at each child's habits, routines, and preferences. How do they interact with one person vs. with a group? Do they interact differently with the therapist than with their parent or with a friend? Do you see different group dynamics for a child in one classroom vs. another? When we use *Culture* to identify strategies to support success, we are looking for tools to support the child within their setting. Consider the following examples:

Individual Culture

- Food preferences and eating habits
- Bedtime routine
    - Fall asleep reading
    - Fall asleep watching TV
    - 4-step bedtime routine visual schedule
- Personal values
- Exercise habits
- Preference for written or verbal communication

Group Culture

- Family meals—sitting at the table every night for dinner
- Family routines
  - Posting a daily visual schedule every morning
  - Running late every morning (adding stress to the morning routine)
- Family holiday rituals
- Religious activities
- Office customs
  - Afternoon tea breaks
  - Working through lunch
  - Friday happy hour
- Classroom routines
  - Zero tolerance for bullying
  - No interruptions when the teacher is talking
  - Encourage question asking and discussion

Reflection

List 3 of your individual cultural preferences:

_____

_____

_____

List 3 groups that influence your social behaviors or expectations (e.g., family, church, school, peers)

_____

_____

_____

How do these groups influence your behavior?

_____

_____

_____

_____

Do any of your behaviors or "cultural norms" change or differ depending on the group you are in at the moment?

_____

_____

_____

_____

_____

Observing and Reflecting on Culture

For therapists reading this book, consider how culture affects participation, engagement, and activity choices (Bonder, Martine, & Miracle, 2004). When we take the time to step back and observe, ask questions, and create goals *with* families or teachers, we can include each child's strengths, values, and preferences. This allows us to create routines or support meaningful habits that will motivate our kids and build success and self-esteem. Coming to these observations with curiosity also gives us the ability to consider our interactions with children and families, reflect on them, and adjust our therapeutic approach when needed.

In fact, occupational therapy can be considered its own culture (Castro, Dahlin-Ivanoff, & Mårtensson, 2014). At STAR Institute, we often talk about our culture in reference to how we emphasize strengths, include parents in intervention, ask questions, encourage reflection, and use A SECRET to create a sensory lifestyle. A SECRET is our way of recognizing these values and working with families to find the best way to translate our professional reasoning process into school and other settings.

For caregivers, thinking about your personal and family culture may take some time and reflection. Consider the following questions and how they impact your culture. What parts of your parenting *Culture* were passed down from your parents? What values come from your family of origin, and how do you purposefully practice the parenting techniques your parents used with you? Do you recognize aspects of your upbringing that you want to change based on your own priorities?

Do relationship-based strategies fit into your family *Culture*, or do you prefer a more traditional behavioral approach? How are you willing and able to adapt with support from a therapist? These are your cultural preferences. It is important to recognize and reflect on what these differences mean to you. How can you make small changes to support your child's success? Which strategies will easily fit into your family *Culture*?

How Does Culture Change?

The belief that *Culture* is dynamic and adaptable may not be familiar to you. But if you reflect on some of your own cultural preferences, you will start to see why we consider it to be flexible. At this point in the book, you already know how much we emphasize relationship and engagement, so it really shouldn't be a surprise that we also see *Culture* as being a relational concept. *Culture* changes precisely because it is relational!

- We are all influenced by our experiences
- Our experiences shape our perceptions
- Each person is an agent of their culture or has the power to change their culture
- Culture is learned through
  - Listening
  - Observing
  - Interacting
  - Reflecting
  - Reflection allows us to evaluate and adapt our culture

When we know that culture is adaptable, we can start to think about pieces that we can change to make ourselves and our kids more successful. Change can be slow, but if we take it one step at a time and recognize that benefits can come from small changes, we know that it can happen!

Bonder, Martin, & Miracle, 2004; Castro, Dahlin-Ivanoff, & Mårtensson, 2014

Reflection

What is one aspect of your personal or chosen family culture that is most important to you?

_____

_____

_____

What is one thing you could change about your personal culture that might support you and your child in becoming more successful?

_____

_____

_____

What small step could you take today to start to make that change in your family culture?

_____

_____

_____

References

Bonder, B. R., Martin, L., & Miracle, A. W. (2004). Culture emergent in occupation. *American Journal of Occupational Therapy, 58,* 159–168.

Castro, D., Dahlin-Ivanoff, S., & Mårtensson, L. (2014). Occupational therapy and culture: a literature review. *Scandinavian Journal of Occupational Therapy, 21*(6), 401–¬414.

On the next page, we provide some examples of *Culture* strategies, or what we call process points. Of course, any of these suggestions should be altered to fit your individual situation. These examples will not fit every child or family but should be used as a guide. The reflection above should help you think about your personal *Culture* and your family or classroom *Culture*. Use the reflection to think about *Culture* process points that will work for you.

A SECRET

Challenge Area	Attunement	Sensation	Emotion Regulation	Culture	Relationship	Environment	Task
				Schedule 1 family sit-down dinner/week	⟳		
			⟳	Set the alarm 15 minutes early on school days (to avoid rushing)			
		⟳		Build 5 minutes of play time into your day (set timer)			⟳
				Commit to exercising for 15 minutes 3 times/week	⟳		
				Create a quiet space where anyone in the family can go when they need to calm down	⟳	⟳	
			⟳	Recognize hand-flapping as your child's need to organize or regulate			
	⟳			Attune to your child's sensory reactions. Use A SECRET to adapt the Environment or provide co-regulation in a stressful situation			
				Post a chore wheel and assign each family member 2 chores/day	⟳		
				Sit down as a family and identify each person's strengths and your family's values			⟳

CHAPTER 9

RELATIONSHIP

R = Relationship

How do we use *Relationship* to support success?

A SECRET							
Challenge Area	Attunement	Sensation	Emotion Regulation	Culture	Relation-ship	Environment	Task

Hopefully, you've noticed by now that *Relationship* plays an essential role in A SECRET. That is because relationships are foundational to human development, not just in early infancy, but throughout the lifespan. In fact, *Relationship* is the cornerstone of self-regulation. So when we want to build self-regulation skills in our children, we need to pay attention to our interactions. This takes time; it takes *Attunement*. It also requires that we practice and strengthen our *Emotion Regulation* capacities so we can co-regulate our kids ⟳.

What Is Relationship?

Our definition of *Relationship* includes connections with specific people (friends, family, or other caregivers). Our brains grow and develop within the context of relationships with our caregivers, loved ones, our larger community, and our environment. When we are in secure and meaningful relationships with others, we can be creative and curious about ourselves and our surroundings (Greenspan & Wieder, 1998, pg 122). From this place of security within *Relationship*, children are able to explore, build independence, and develop self-esteem.

Relationship refers to not only our connections with specific people, but also our *capacity* to engage with others. Our social engagement system allows us to have positive interactions with individuals or in groups, supports a feeling of physical connection with others, and creates a feeling of safety in that connection (Porges & Carter, 2017). Remember that our brains are wired to connect with others. It is essential that we help our children understand the importance of developing strong relationships (Siegel & Payne, 2012). Having support systems and the ability to engage others' support is one of the essential components of resilience. So we use *Relationship* strategies to support regulation, create a feeling of safety, and build resilience in our children.

We all know it's impossible to stay connected and positive all the time. Don't worry; relationships are not in jeopardy when we yell, slam the door, or feel disconnected from our kids. The most important thing is the connection or repair that comes after a meltdown or a loss of connection. The repair with your child (or in any relationship) actually grows stronger connections in the brain and offering opportunities to build resilience (Siegel & Payne, 2012). This is also when reasoning may actually be able to happen—when you and your child can reflect back on the incident and consider the other person's feelings.

Social-Emotional Development

We look at the development of social-emotional skills (including self-regulation) through the lens of DIR/Floortime—the work of Drs. Stanley Greenspan and Serena Wieder (1998). Through this lens, we don't view the development of self-regulation as a capacity that grows in isolation, but as one that grows within relationship. Our capacity to connect with another person in early infancy with our primary caregivers provides the foundation for self-regulation and, from there, higher-level skills and abilities. In typical development, infants already have some ability to monitor and regulate their capacity for social interactions. We see infants turn away or avert their gaze when eye contact becomes too intense. They may suck their thumbs to try to regulate and respond to the intense sensory information that comes with social engagement. For our kids with SPD, that same level of engagement may be quickly dysregulating, *and* they don't have the same capacity to down regulate when they are overwhelmed (see chapter 3).

Relationship and SPD

Dr. Daniel Siegel (2012) refers to relationships as "the sharing of energy and information flow," meaning the processing and integrating of sensory information, the information that comes from engaging with others. Think of the energy it takes just to make eye contact for an extended period of time. For some of us, this is easy; we actually gain energy from engaging with other people. But for others, social engagement can be draining. These individual differences are partly based on personality or temperament styles but are also very much dependent on our sensory differences.

We need to attune to each child's individual differences and recognize what helps them connect with others. For children who are over-responsive to visual, auditory, or tactile information, engaging with another person can be overwhelming and dysregulating. It may be almost painful to make eye contact or shake hands with another person. Children with dyspraxia may feel awkward in social situations, while sensory cravers may not be able to get enough engagement. Sensory under-responsiveness may require that we increase our affect and proximity to engage children. Parents, teachers, and caregivers may need to shift their expectations of neuro-normative social interactions and find ways that children with SPD can feel safe connecting with others.

In this chapter we will think about how we use children's strengths to support their ability to make social connections. Who are the most empathetic and caring people in your child's life? What supports can we provide to make our children more successful in social interactions?

And what expectations should we have regarding our children's interactions and relationships? Chapter 3 details the importance of early social interactions for stimulating brain growth and developing self-regulation—refer back to chapter 3 to reflect on using *Relationship* strategies to support your child.

Relationship in OT Intervention

> In typical development, just-right balance in the moment comes naturally. For our children with SPD, it can require work. A skillful therapist uses the therapeutic relationship, attuning to the child's individual sensory differences, to find the just-right success. It looks like the therapist is "just playing," because play is the work. Connection, or Relationship, is the therapy.
>
> "In play, the players explore the dynamic space—the play— between order and disorder, reordering and rebalancing themselves in relationship to the experience and to other players, finding the just-right balance in the moment."
>
> Hewes, 2014

There are many OT activities to address sensory and motor development, but for children, therapy should look like play. It is playing in *Relationship* that creates a sense of safety for our children with SPD (Wagner, 2015). *Relationship* and sense of safety allow real learning to occur. A highly trained therapist will skillfully use all of the elements of A SECRET to support the therapeutic relationship and help a child feel successful. As discussed in Chapter 3, the *Relationship* allows the child to explore, take risks, and build self-regulation. The therapist reads the child's verbal and non-verbal cues to build connection. Ideally, the therapist will then pass on this magic to the parent. The therapeutic relationship is important, but ultimately the child's relationship with their primary caregiver is the most important!

Relationship in the Schools

OTs in the school system can play an essential role in using *Relationship* strategies to support learning. This includes identifying a child's strengths and individual sensory differences, then putting specific strategies into place. Recommendations should include finding supportive relationships and helping children.

Relationship Strategies in Schools

- Identify a "safe person" for connection when your child is dysregulated
- Take a minute to get on a child's level and offer empathy
- Offer genuine and specific praise
- Provide self-regulation strategies for the entire classroom (don't single students out)
- Help children recognize their sensory needs
- Create a plan for self-advocacy
- Use a buddy system for independent work time or transitions between classes

- Create a *Culture* of connection and community (Schaber, 2015)
- Make space for students' voices (Hammond, 2014)
- Use classroom routines *(Task)* to support a *Culture* of learning (Hammond, 2015)

Educators also recognize the importance of *Relationship* in creating a supportive environment for learning. "Relational Learning" and "Caring Curriculums" are being promoted in some school districts, from elementary school through college (Battaglia, 2016; Schaber, 2014) While teachers may have limited time to build individual relationships with students, it is possible to support students' capacities for connectedness with a focus on *Relationship* and community. Teachers can build safe learning environments or learning partnerships through relationship-focused humanistic teaching practices (Hammond, 2015; Schaber, 2014). When educators lead with a *Culture* of kindness, respect, and patience, listening to students' needs and interests, they can promote healthy risk-taking and active involvement in the learning process ⬡. This can be especially important for children with SPD, who often learn best in non-traditional ways.

Developing Self-Regulation through Relationships

We've mentioned co-regulation many times throughout this book, because it is a powerful way of affecting another person's emotion regulation. *Co-regulation* refers to the bi-directional process that occurs in relationships. We can consciously attempt to co-regulate another person to help them maintain a regulated state, but it is more often an unconscious process that works in both directions. We may want to "downregulate" (calm down) a child who is upset, but their dysregulation has an effect on us too! How often do you find yourself becoming "too fast" when you are interacting with your upset child? These are the moments that we need to work on our own emotion regulation before we can support our children.

Let's look at a few examples of co-regulation in this book. Lacey in chapter 13 is overly sensitive, both physiologically and emotionally. Her sensory system becomes more dysregulated when she is required by COVID-19 restrictions to see her therapist online instead of face-to-face. Her therapist is trying to find a way to make Lacey less afraid and to get her back to the level she was at when they worked together before COVID-19 in real life. Her OT realized that play time at home should allow Lacey to have fun and connect with others, making her feel successful in *Relationship*. Secondly, her OT allowed Lacey, when online, to play a game typical of a much younger child. This again reinforced Lacey's success and self-esteem and resulted in Lacey being more willing to turn on the video again.

There are many techniques to co-regulate a child, but the key is this: you must check in on your own arousal level to make sure you yourself are regulated before trying any of these techniques. True co-regulation is sensing unconsciously that your partner, leader, or collaborator is truly calm, and almost no one can make themselves seem regulated when they are not. Regulation is a low-level response that you can't trick your brain out of. It takes practice to recognize and respond when your arousal is high, and it's even harder when you are reaching the point of dysregulation. In times of emotional distress, the "thinking brain" (cerebral cortex) goes "offline," which explains in part why a strong emotional reaction can override any logical thought (Siegel, 2012). This is not the time to try to reason with your child, but it is a time to connect. That may mean just being present and often using minimal to no language. Just be there to support, and be ready to connect and repair when your child is calm.

Cindy's Story

How can we use *Relationship* to help Cindy at recess?

Cindy, a second-grader, struggles at recess. Today, she sits alone and watches the other girls running around the field, laughing and having fun. Cindy looks down and talks to her imaginary friend, Alice. She says, "Alice, I hate recess, what about you? No one ever plays with us." Ms. Janet, Cindy's OT, has noted that she sits at recess for 45 minutes every day but never engages with other kids.

> Miss Janet has made arrangements to use 30 minutes twice a day observing recess, because she has found that it is not only a great way to screen kids for sensory, motor, and relationship issues, but also a non-threatening way to treat children.

Ms. Janet asks Cindy if there is something that looks like fun to her on the playground. She asks about the monkey bars or maybe the slide. Cindy says, "We are not scared of those stupid monkey bars, right,

Alice? Going down the slide is so dumb; we would never do that, right?"

Just then one of the teacher assistants shouts out to Cindy, "Cindy, go join the other girls! Run and play with them."

Cindy responds by whispering quietly to her special friend Alice, "No, we think they are stupid!" and begins to cry. Cindy says, "Why doesn't anyone understand how we feel, Alice?"

Ms. Janet, Cindy's OT, is on the playground to observe the kids at recess as usual. "Hi, Cindy," Ms. Janet says. Cindy responds, "Say 'hi' to Alice, too!"

"Oh," Ms. Janet responds, "sometimes I forget she is there with you! Hi, Cindy, and hi, Alice."

"Can I join you?" asks Janet. Cindy says, "Sure, we were just saying how dumb recess time is! We don't want any part of it."

Ms. Janet understands that Cindy feels alone and has created an imaginary friend, Alice, to support her during challenging situations. Cindy often sits by herself during social events, not only during recess, but also during lunch. Ms. Janet is trying to understand why Cindy feels so lonely.

What purpose does Alice fulfill for Cindy? Obviously, Cindy has created someone whom she can control in her imagination, someone who will let her just sit and watch without interfering. Cindy needs that support full-time since she feels insecure. Alice "understands" Cindy's point of view and never pushes her out of her comfort zone. Alice doesn't ask Cindy to go down the slide (which she is afraid of) or talk about her thoughts and feelings, which Cindy says "is a total waste of time." Cindy constructed Alice because Alice can help her feel better about herself during these trying moments that make her want to kick the wall or hide from the world.

Ms. Janet didn't know if it was okay to reinforce Cindy's fantasy or if it was better to try to make her face reality. She and the social worker spent some time talking about the importance of Cindy facing reality (that Alice was a fantasy figure and not real) and the possibility of using Alice to help Cindy face her challenges. Ms. Jaime wondered if the good part of having Cindy regulate her emotions was worth agreeing to play along with her made-up friend. They worked out a plan to support Cindy's fantasy for a few weeks but to try to wean her off the need for Alice by figuring out what other students she might be able to make friends with. Meanwhile, the teacher offered emotional support. (Of course, her teacher must be brought into the loop, and Ms. Janet and the social worker are hoping to talk to her soon to figure out what role the teacher wants to play; they discussed making sure the plan is okay with the teacher and finding out the extent to which the teacher prefers to be involved herself vs. having the OT handle it during recess.)

Janet says to Cindy and Alice, "Let's think of some things we can do during recess that would be fun."

Cindy responds, "Well, I love drawing and painting, and so does Alice." Janet smiles and says, "Me too. That's cool. How about I go inside and get some of my art supplies for you guys? Would you like that?

Cindy feels that Janet is really connected to her and is willing to take the time to understand what she wants. Janet is collaborating with Cindy, and together they are forming a plan of an activity that will be enjoyable. Ms. Janet says, "I will be right back. I am going to bring out some paper, colored pencils and a few clipboards to lean on. Is that okay with you, Cindy?" Cindy is smiling and feeling better.

The first part of this vignette demonstrates how every-thing that happens in a person's life can represent many of the A SECRET elements. In this story, Cindy has an important pretend relationship with her doll. She uses her pretending with Alice as a way to stay regulated when times seem difficult at home and at school. Note also that the context is quite important to Cindy. When she is at home, so is her imaginary friend, but at school she is not able to use her imaginary friend for emotion regulation very often. The other children make fun of her for pretending that she has an imaginary friend. They call her "baby" and "'fraidy-cat" for not wanting to run around and play like they do. either has to either hide her friend or rely on being co-regulated by her teacher, her OT, or another staff member. To staff members who do not understand Cindy's need for Alice, Cindy may seem "needy" or "immature" or just "whiny."

When Janet returns with the art supplies, she asks, "What should I draw?"

Cindy responds, "Ms. Janet, what are you going to draw?"

"You can draw anything you want. This is your special drawing time."

Cindy, smiling, is relieved that the expectation of this activity will be based on her ideas. She asks Janet, "Can you sit with me and draw while I draw?"

"Of course, and thank you for including me," says Ms. Janet.

Here, we see how a potentially disastrous situation with Cindy continuing to feel lonely and isolated could be changed. It didn't take much of an effort for Ms. Janet to help Cindy feel understood. She stopped and listened to what Cindy was saying and thought about what Cindy might be feeling. She communicated with Cindy, and together they collaborated to create a plan. Cindy felt that Janet supported her, especially when she acknowledged Alice, Cindy's imaginary friend,

Now the current crisis had been resolved, and the two remaining issues became:

1. How and whether to deal with Cindy's possible over-responsivity to vestibular stimulation (i.e., the "stupid" slide and not 'liking' the monkey bars)

2. How and when to deal with Alice, Cindy's imaginary friend

Cindy is smiling because she feels relieved that the performance expectations are left to her. It didn't take much effort for Miss Janet to help Cindy feel understood. She used the little mantra "Stop, look, and listen" to connect with Cindy and put herself in Cindy's shoes; she did capture the feelings, leaving Cindy decidedly more comfortable than she had been previously. Because Janet took the time to communicate and collaborate with Cindy, they were able to create a plan together.

In terms of dealing with Cindy's imaginary friend, Janet, with the help of the team's social worker, decided there were two possibilities. It could be that this friend was a totally benign helper that Cindy fabricated but really didn't believe was there. In that scenario, Cindy would easily separate reality from fantasy but use the fantasy to support herself as needed. In the second scenario, Cindy would not be able to "give up" Alice because she would believe that Alice was actually real. This could be a sign of a more serious problem that should be handled by an outside service provider, probably a psychiatrist. It would take a few weeks to determine which applied to Cindy, but they would proceed with the assumption that the first scenario applied. If Cindy hung onto Alice beyond what seemed reasonable for a second-grader, they would re-discuss with the rest of the team (including her teacher and parents) and refer her to the appropriate care provider. They agreed to meet in three weeks to touch base, and meanwhile Janet would proceed with figuring out whether Cindy believed Alice was real.

Using the framework of A SECRET, let's take a closer look at Cindy:

Cindy's challenges became problematic when the assistant teacher asked Cindy to join other students at recess.

1. **Attunement:** Was the assistant teacher attuned to Cindy? Was Cindy accepting of the information received from the assistant teacher? What might have been a more successful way to suggest that Cindy go play with the other girls?

2. **Sensation:** At this time and probably every time the class goes to the playground, Cindy has a "fight or flight" response to the overstimulating visual and auditory input on the playground. Because Cindy is also has a tactile over-responsivity, she sees the playground as potentially dangerous.

What would you recommend doing encourage Cindy to feel safe in this setting? How can sensation be used to influence Cindy in this context? Figure 10.1 provides ideas for helpful sensation ideas divided by type of sensory stimuli from which a child might benefit.

RELATIONSHIP-BASED SUPPORTS: MODULATION (LOWER LEVEL) AND COGNITIVE (HIGHER LEVEL)

Targeting Lower Brain Levels Sensory Over-Responsivity	Targeting Higher Brain Levels Sensory Discrimination
Vestibular over-responsivity: Cindy is afraid to go on the playground equipment or have her feet leave the ground. Ms. Janet will sit on the grass with Cindy during this rock painting activity. As they get more involved in forming a relationship together, swinging with her feet touching the ground as they explore different options of what designs they can paint may be incorporated.	*Proprioception:* Difficulty interpreting characteristics of sensory stimuli experienced through the use of muscles and joints.
Tactile over-responsivity: Cindy does not enjoy participating in group activities and is uncomfortable with the thought of working with peers who may bump into her and cause her to trip. She is much "safer" working with an adult who is more predictable and is creating a plan for them to follow.	*Tactile:* Difficulty interpreting characteristics of sensory stimuli that is felt on skin. Experience and practice drawing shapes on skin, in shaving cream and other textures. Also, recognize shapes and letters by feeling them, not by seeing them; hide them in sand or put them in a cloth bag and have the child feel to find a certain letter.

RELATIONSHIP-BASED SUPPORTS: MODULATION (LOWER LEVEL) AND COGNITIVE (HIGHER LEVEL)

Targeting Lower Brain Levels Sensory Over-Responsivity	Targeting Higher Brain Levels Sensory Discrimination
Social-emotional Very reactive to being on the playground. Cries when she is asked to play with the girls who are using the equipment, running, and loudly conversing.	*Social-emotional:* Experiences many emotions. Quite emotionally labile. Play game where emotion labeling is the point of game.
Auditory: Use a soft voice and short sentences, and DON'T talk too much! Listen to soft music with lower frequencies. Use soft music, a white-noise machine, or relaxing environmental sounds on CD with nature sounds. Wear earmuffs or ear plugs. Use noise-cancellaing headphones or other headphones, but do not force the child to use earphones. The child should be exposed to various kinds of music. Do not isolate the child from unexpected sounds, e.g., fireworks, loud car mufflers, sirens. Instead, work with them during the stimuli with whichever strategy works.	*Auditory:* Work with auditory tasks, such as writing down the numbers you say with a tape playing music in the background, or inviting the class to chat at a low level to distract from discrimination tasks. Make this fun and funny! It will still give the child an opportunity to practice differentiating foreground sound from background sounds.

Discussion: Using the framework of A SECRET, let's take a closer look at this story.

1. Attunement

Miss Janet is able to attune to Cindy and offer empathy, which makes Cindy feel connected. Since Cindy is essentially a compliant, quiet girl, her teachers have not realized the extent of her insecurities. Miss Janet knows that Cindy loves art project and connects easily with this preferred activity. Miss Janet also acknowledged and accepted Alice, Cindy's imaginary friend.

2. Sensation

Miss Janet is aware of Cindy's sensory over-responsivities, but she has also identified sensory supports that help Cindy stay regulated. Creating a recess schedule *with* Cindy provides structure and opportunities for calming and organizing input. Cindy goes to recess with: 1) a visual schedule, 2) preferred exercises that offer heavy work (proprioceptive) input, 3) visual boundaries using chalk and poly spots (so Cindy knows she won't be bumped by other children), 4) a five-minute visual timer, and 5) structured sensory-motor play with a small group of girls.

3. Emotion Regulation

How can we help Cindy so that recess is truly a break and not another sensory challenge? When Cindy was asked to join the other girls, she was overwhelmed and wasn't offered any structure. There are a few options to support Cindy's emotion regulation. There are two recess periods per day at Cindy's school, so Miss Janet requests that Cindy only attend one recess per day. Miss Janet knows Cindy responds well to structure, so she works with Cindy and her teacher to set up a regular routine with a visual schedule.

4. Culture

Changing the expectation to one recess each day is a positive cultural shift for Cindy. Ms. Janet speaks to Cindy's parents to create a plan for movement opportunities that are more supportive for her. She is much more successful with social interactions in an environment that is less stimulating and that has regular routines and repetition.

5. Relationship

Miss Janet can't be with Cindy at every recess, but she has identified many strategies to support Cindy's social interactions. Recognizing Cindy's individual sensory differences allows Cindy to feel supported and successful in peer relationships.

Reflection

Pay attention to your own arousal level when your child is frustrated, upset, or melting down. What do you do to keep yourself regulated so you can co-regulate? (Sometimes the first step is just paying attention! We know it's hard to stay regulated during meltdowns.)

_____

_____

_____

_____

_____

_____

_____

_____

Watch how your child responds to language when they are upset. Does it help when you stop talking or limit your language? Or does your child need words to provide structure?

_____

_____

_____

_____

_____

_____

_____

_____

How do you feel after you have a playful or connected moment with your child? What words would you use to describe the feeling?

_____

_____

_____

_____

_____

_____

What does your child need from you when they are upset? Do they do better with distance and alone time, or do they prefer to have you close by?

_____

_____

_____

_____

_____

_____

_____

_____

_____

If it feels difficult to connect with your child, what tools/strategies can you use from other elements of A SECRET to support your relationship? What *Environment* is most comforting for you both? What sensory tools help your child (and you) stay organized and regulated? Can you schedule regular play sessions/reading time/walks/etc. to connect with your child (*Culture*)?

_____

_____

_____

_____

_____

_____

_____

_____

_____

References

Battaglia, J. (2016). Toward a Caring Curriculum: Can Occupational Therapy Be Taught in a Caring Context? *International Journal of Teaching and Learning in Higher Education,* 28(2), 265-270.

Greenspan, S. I., Wieder, S., & Simons, R. (1998). *The Child with Special Needs: Encouraging Intellectual and Emotional Growth.* Addison-Wesley/Addison Wesley Longman.

Hammond, Z. (2014). *Culturally Responsive Teaching and the Brain: Promoting Authentic Engagement and Rigor among Culturally and Linguistically Diverse Students.* Corwin Press.

Hewes, J. (2014). Seeking balance in motion: The role of spontaneous free play in promoting social and emotional health in early childhood care and education. *Children, 1*(3), 280-301.

Porges, S. W., & Carter, C. S. (2017). Polyvagal theory and the social engagement system. Complementary and Integrative Treatments in Psychiatric Practice. Washington, DC: *American Psychiatric Association Publishing,* 221-241.

Schaber, P. (2014). Conference Proceedings—Keynote address: Searching for and identifying signature pedagogies in occupational therapy education. *American Journal of Occupational Therapy, 68,* S40–S44. http://dx.doi.org/10.5014/ ajot.2014.685S08

Siegel, D. J. (2012). *Pocket Guide to Interpersonal Neurobiology: An Integrative Handbook of the Mind (Norton Series on Interpersonal Neurobiology).* WW Norton & Company.

Siegel, D. J., & Bryson, T. P. (2012). *The Whole-Brain Child: 12 Revolutionary Strategies to Nurture Your Child's Developing Mind.* Bantam.

Wagner, D. (2015). Polyvagal theory and peek-a-boo: How the therapeutic pas de deux heals attachment trauma. Body, *Movement and Dance in Psychotherapy*, 10(4), 256-265.

On the next page, we provide some examples of *Relationship* strategies, or what we call process points. Of course, any of these suggestions should be altered to fit your individual situation. These examples will not fit every child or family but should be used as a guide. Use the reflection to think about *Relationship* process points that will work for you.

A SECRET

Challenge Area	Attunement	Sensation	Emotion Regulation	Culture	Relationship	Environment	Task
		⟳			• Use strategies to build self-confidence: – Call attention to strengths – Give one step at a time for multi-step tasks – Stay calm		
			⟳		• Identify a "safe person" at school who can: – Slow pace of voice – Limit voice volume – Stay in close proximity (down on child's level) – Provide gentle deep pressure input (to shoulders, back)		
					• Adjust expectation of eye contact & other neuro-normative social interactions		
			⟳		• Schedule regular one-on-one playtime – Follow child's lead in play		⟳
					• Give specific positive praise (what was done and how)		
					• Use your body to create a safe space (down on child's level, child's back to stimulating environment, attune & provide physical support as needed)	⟳	
					• Acknowledge and encourage ideas, providing support for organization		⟳

190

CHAPTER 10

ENVIRONMENT

E = Environment

How do we use Environment to support success?

A SECRET							
Challenge Area	Attunement	Sensation	Emotion Regulation	Culture	Relation-ship	Environment	Task

Environment refers to the setting that makes up the current circumstances of our surroundings. Using this definition, *Environment* may involve physical surroundings or social factors, including objects and people in our immediate vicinity. It may even refer to the attitudes and actions of people in close proximity. Depending on our ability to process sensory information, we may perceive the environment very differently from someone standing right next to us.

Environment is a factor that is often considered by occupational therapists. Adapting the environment to help children participate in daily activities is a central goal of OT intervention. We assess environmental factors and consider how individuals function within specific contexts. We also identify environmental barriers and suggest adaptations to support independence.

Looking at the element of *Environment* in A SECRET provides an opportunity to consider how surroundings affect behavior in both supportive and challenging ways. We can recognize what might be overwhelming about certain environments and try to avoid putting children into dysregulating situations. With *Environment*, we also problem-solve strategies to help children be successful in challenging contexts. Because we include both physical and social factors in *Environment*, strategies in this element usually interact with other elements of A SECRET, especially *Sensation*.

Recognizing environmental issues usually means attuning to sensory aspects of your child's surroundings and their individual sensory needs. For instance, the grocery store may be loud and visually overstimulating, especially at the busiest time of day. Shopping during off-hours may be a simple way to adapt the environment to support your child. Some children thrive in outdoor spaces, so they may be more successful engaging with friends at a birthday party in the park. Providing sensory supports to decrease visual and auditory input at a baseball game (sunglasses, baseball cap, and headphones) may help your child enjoy a family outing.

Create an Environment That Supports the Child's Success

Let's think about a concrete example of environmental adaptations, in this case, modifying the environment to make it wheelchair-accessible. If the doorway is too narrow, a wheelchair assists a person in moving through the doorway. To resolve this barrier, the door entrance needs to be adapted so that the width accommodates the wheelchair's pass-through. When an adult leaves a hospital setting and has a number of physical impairments that alter their participation in the home environment, the occupational therapist can assess the areas of physical, cognitive and emotional challenges and create modifications to the home that optimize function and performance. Changing and altering the environment to meet the needs of the individual can maximize performance in daily occupations. For kids with SPD, we usually modify their environments to make them more sensory-friendly.

If you ask all of the student's teachers about how they perform in classrooms, you will probably get a number of different responses. You are talking about the same child who performs very differently depending on the environment and context. If the child is very sensitive to movement, the child may have behaviors that stand out in physical education classes. For a child who is over-responsive to auditory input, music class, the lunchroom, or the auditorium may present significant difficulty.

Sunlight, wind, playground equipment, plants, birds and other natural elements in the environment may be calming for children with SPD.

For some children, outdoor breaks may facilitate engagement in fun activities with friends on the playground, while for others this environment may be overwhelming.

As with every other element of A SECRET, there is no one answer for how to adapt the *Environment*. It is necessary to pay attention to your child's individual sensory differences, perhaps have an OT assess their specific sensory needs, and always remember to observe and ask questions. Of course, this is where A SECRET will come in handy!

Interventions can address sensory processing to promote self-regulation in preparation for social participation. This approach may involve active participation of the student through use of simulated components as in a "sensory gym." Through movement, tactile sensations, scents, and other environmental supplements, optimum levels of arousal are promoted and the student may be more alert before engaging in a classroom activity. Occupational therapists often consult with business and community sites to establish sensory-friendly environments for individuals with sensory processing challenges.

Let's look at some specific examples of the environment and its impact on learning and attention. *Environment* can be described as a milieu that makes up the site-specific setting. It refers to actual physical surroundings that can be found in a specific context.

- Graetz (2006) describes the psychology of learning environments by linking the physical characteristics to their emotional effects on learners with cognitive and behavioral issues. She describes issues that relate directly to classroom learning, such as loud noise, the ability to obtain adequate arousal states, sitting and positioning in different chairs while learning, and the number of visual distractions that are present, all of which produce varying challenges for certain student learners.

- Chellappa et al. (2011) provide evidence that light in the environment can enhance an individual's focus. They examine the effect of enriched light on melatonin suppression, alertness, and cognitive performance.
- Reilly, Donkelaar, Saavedra and Woolacott (2008) demonstrate the interaction of attention with posture and movement. Physical activity was effective in the sample studied in improving task behavior during classroom instruction.

Environmental issues are external to the individual and may or may not influence all of the student's behaviors and emotions. Note in the following story about Tomas how the teacher and occupational therapist implement creative environmental modifications to help Tomas succeed.

Using A SECRET to Support Tomas in the Classroom Environment

Ms. Zinn, Tomas' teacher, is proud of his progress in following the directions of the task he is working on. Unfortunately, many of the students are taking a long time to finish up. Now, nearly 20 minutes into the activity, Tomas is getting fidgety and antsy. Ms. Zinn is an open-minded teacher and has decided to consult with the OT, who may be able to suggest some modifications in the classroom environment to support Tomas. The OT makes some suggestions for adaptive seating. Instead of being seated straightforward in a traditional chair, she suggests that Tomas, and any other children who might benefit from these, use Chair Moves, a program of five chair positions that provides increased sensation while staying seated. This *Sensation*  strategy can be helpful for children who struggle in a busy classroom environment.

Ms. Zinn posts pictures of the positions on the wall for the children to see. Of the five positions, Tomas chooses position 1 in the Chair Moves sequence and places his chair so that the back of it faces his desk while he straddles the chair (see Figure 10.1). Tomas sits without back support and uses his core strength to sit upright. Movement and proprioception are inherent to this position and help change his arousal state so he can regulate himself while waiting for the other children to finish the task.

Figure 10.1

The chair moves work for a few minutes, but Ms. Zinn sees that Tomas starts talking to his neighbors and look over the Audrey's shoulder, since she is sitting next to him. Ms. Zinn asks if Tomas can think of other ideas to stay calm while the other children finish the task. Ms. Zinn tries to increase his independence and awareness of when he needs to switch to a new strategy. Tomas decides to try position 2 of Chair Moves. Ms. Zinn can see that Tomas is well on his way to interrupting Audrey but notices that as Tomas turns his chair sideways for position 2, the chair back creates a built-in

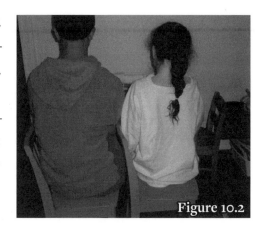

Figure 10.2

visual and physical boundary between Tomas and Audrey (Figure 10.2).

Next, Ms. Zinn asks everyone to share their project with the buddy sitting next to them. Notice how she simultaneously considers relationship and environment. Ms. Zinn praises Tomas for his great idea in using Chair Moves and asks all the children to use Position 2 of chair moves for the next part of the activity.

The children will share crayons and glue and use Chair Moves to help them to stay within their own space by setting a concrete boundary. Now, every set of two children can share the materials happily and giggle together while completing the task.

Simple modifications (such as placing tape on either side of a child's desk that no one else is allowed to cross and using stickers to differentiate spatial boundaries and personal space) can make an enormous difference in the way children perceive their own and others' personal space. Not getting into other people's faces and spaces can make a huge difference in being accepted by peers. Often environmental modifications are helpful when socializing with peers.

Another technique that involves use of the environment is teaching students to provide themselves with soothing activities that the environment they are in can help with. One tool is to teach students how to "push the wall down." Encourage them to find a corner of a spare room (maybe the boys'/girls' room) and take a minute to push their back against two walls. This provides extra proprioception and increases a sense of safety and security,

Methods like having "time-in" and pushing against walls in a corner cost nothing and are simple for children to understand. While cues may be needed, kids will take a big step toward self-regulation if they can seek out places of refuge rather than striking out, having a temper tantrum, or fleeing. Obviously, every child and every situation is different. There are a multitude of activities that you can use to soothe your child before or after they are feeling over-aroused.

It's the thinking process that we're trying to convey here, not the specific activities! You need to know how to think about the students' struggles and ask the right questions so you can figure out environmental strategies that might be useful to your child at home or at school during their challenged times.

Examples of Simple *Environment* Strategies

- Putting a cushion on a child's chair to provide movement opportunities in the classroom
- Sitting on a wobble stool
- Using a ball chair instead of a traditional classroom chair to increase attention

- Dimming the lights in the classroom or using light filters to cover the fluorescent lighting
- Placing tape on either side of a child's desk to delineate personal space
- Using stickers to differentiate spatial boundaries
- Sitting on carpet squares for circle time
- Lining up on numbers on the floor to space children out evenly
- Consider placement in the classroom
    - Next to the teacher for children who need more support
    - Front of the room to cut out visual input for children with discrimination challenges
    - Back of the room for children who benefit from more visual stimulation to maintain the just-right arousal level
- Placement in an organized and structured classroom for a child with dyspraxia

Environmental Adaptations to Support Stewart's Postural Challenges

Stewart is a bright, friendly, seven-year-old boy with SPD. His postural challenges make it difficult for him to join in sports with peers, and he desperately wants to play volleyball with his friends. He also struggles to stay seated, and therefore pay attention, during homework time. It is our job to create strategies that will support Stewart in finding ways that he can be successful with homework and volleyball (or to find other ways that he can join his friends in play). (Just a side note here: anything a child *really* wants to do is generally worth trying, because he will be so motivated!)

Stewart's parents and his OT identified that one of the barriers to playing volleyball is the environment. Because of his postural challenges, Stewart has difficulty maintaining balance and postural control on the uneven surface of the volleyball court at school. He is also easily fatigued by moving through such a large space. His parents started by changing the environment in their basement. They cleared a section of the room so the family could play volleyball there. The stable surface was easier for Stewart to handle, and the smaller space meant he didn't have to move as much during the game. He started playing with his family in this environment, then invited some friends over as he gained more confidence. Eventually, Stewart was able to play with his friends on the volleyball court in the neighborhood park. Instead of shifting positions, Stewart stayed in the same position throughout most of the game. His parents limited the distance he had to move by drawing a chalk-line boundary, where he played during most of the game.

Stewart's parents recognized that his desk was in a quiet corner of the room with limited stimulation. They thought this would be the perfect environment for studying. They also found a chair that promoted an upright posture, but Stewart often slumped in the chair and leaned forward onto his desk. The environment was modified to support Stewart's sensory under-responsivity (which is commonly associated with postural challenges). To increase visual stimulation (and improve his arousal level), his parents moved Stewart's desk so he faced out the window, where he had more light and more movement in his visual field. This initially seemed counterproductive, but Stewart needed the increased input. To support his posture and stability, his OT provided a cushion that provided a slight amount of movement and improved Stewart's position in the chair. He rotated between sitting and standing with a standing desk.

There are endless ways to modify the environment to support children with challenges in any SPD subtype. Use the following reflection questions to think about how the environment might be changed to support your child.

Reflection

What sensory characteristics make up your child's favorite environment?

_____

_____

_____

_____

_____

_____

_____

_____

Describe the environment where your child is most successful with completing tasks:

_____

_____

_____

_____

_____

_____

_____

_____

Describe the environment where it seems easiest for your child to engage with others:

_____

_____

_____

_____

_____

_____

_____

_____

_____

What environments are most challenging for your child? Which sensory characteristics seem most difficult for your child (or most dysregulating)?

_____

_____

_____

_____

_____

_____

_____

_____

What type of environment is most calming for your child? What sensory tools could you add to a quiet space for your child?

_____

_____

_____

_____

_____

_____

_____

_____

References

Chellappa, S. L., Steiner, R., Blattner, P., Oelhafen, P., Götz, T., & Cajochen, C. (2011). Non-visual effects of light on melatonin, alertness and cognitive performance: can blue-enriched light keep us alert? *PloS One, 6*(1), e16429.

Graetz, K. A. (2006). The psychology of learning environments. *Educause Review, 41*(6), 60-75.

Reilly, D. S., van Donkelaar, P., Saavedra, S., & Woollacott, M. H. (2008). Interaction between the development of postural control and the executive function of attention. *Journal of Motor Behavior, 40*(2), 90-102.

On the next page, we provide some examples of *Environment* strategies, or what we call process points. Of course, any of these suggestions should be altered to fit your individual situation. These examples will not fit every child or family but should be used as a guide. Use the reflection to think about *Environment* process points that will work for you.

A SECRET

Challenge Area	Attunement	Sensation	Emotion Regulation	Culture	Relationship	Environment	Task
				⟳		• Organize workspace to improve attention	

			⟳			• Create a safe space to calm down or sharing feelings
						  – Quiet corner
						  – Bean bag or crash pad
						  – Favorite blanket or stuffed animal
						  – Fidgets/preferred toys	

			⟳	⟳		• Discuss challenges of specific environments and make a plan (with your child) to support regulation	

	⟳					• Provide a predictability in unfamiliar environments
						  – visual schedule
						  – create routine	

		⟳				• Decrease clutter in homework area	
		⟳				• Place important items directly in visual field	⟳
			⟳			• Use your own body to create a small space. Find a corner or a wall where you can sit (your back against the wall) & have your child face you to cut out the busy environment	

CHAPTER 11

TASK

T = Task

How do we use Task to support success?

Challenge Area	Attunement	Sensation	Emotion Regulation	Culture	Relation-ship	Environment	Task

A SECRET

As occupational therapists, we are trained to break down and analyze tasks. We consider all of the aspects of a task (physical, social, cognitive, emotional). We break down the number of steps involved in completing a task and think about the goals related to task completion. We could go on...but we aren't going to ask you to do that here! However, we will spend some time thinking about tasks, because this element is essential to supporting kids with SPD. While *Task* seems like one of the most straightforward elements of A SECRET, it may not be as simple as it seems. Remember that in each element we always consider both strengths and challenges. So, with *Task*, we first want to think about activities that make a child feel successful. What tasks do they enjoy doing? What tasks help them calm down? What tasks can they enjoy with another person to build trust and strengthen relationships?

We also have to consider the challenges that come with certain tasks. When do we need to decrease our expectations? When do sensory challenges make it more difficult to complete what seems like a simple task? How many steps does the task have? How much support does a child need? Would they be more successful with visual supports, written instructions, demonstration, or modeling instead of verbal instructions? There is a lot to think about for this element, and this chapter will help you problem-solve how to make your child successful with participation in non-preferred tasks, recognize why some tasks are so difficult for your child, and how to use tasks to support your child in different situations.

Task is essential to A SECRET! As with every element of A SECRET, we are always thinking of how each element flows into the next and how they are all connected. When we understand and attune to our kids' preferences, the context or environment they are in, their emotional state, and their current sensory challenges, we can adjust the task to support them in the moment. We want our kids to be successful and build confidence, so we want tasks to be at the just-right level. Kids should be successful but also challenged just enough to keep them engaged and interested in the task.

Below is an example of how we helped a family use *Task* to support their child's development of emotion regulation skills.

Natalie and Ron Smith came to a parent education session and described frequent stressful and embarrassing situations in which their son, Mathias, threw a fit every time they needed to shop in the grocery store or do anything else necessary for the survival of the family. Mathias ran the show, they said. It was his way or no way. The Smiths had no insight into what triggered Mathias' meltdowns.

Our OT, Jamie, talked to his parents about how the effects of sensations could accumulate throughout the day until some mild stimulus served as the straw that broke that camel's back. She also helped them problem-solve how to determine how much sensory stimulation Mathias could tolerate. They discussed strategies to help him to function best when, say, a trip to the grocery store was unavoidable. You will see how this discussion of the just-right task and calming sensory strategies led to ideas for other elements of A SECRET. Once you start thinking this way it all flows together, creating a *sensory lifestyle*!

Jamie could have given Natalie and Ron a list of activities to try. But she didn't. Instead, her goal was to teach them how to think about what their son might need *in the moment*. Jamie suggested they try some of our active problem-solving techniques. We've found that teaching caretakers how to ask the "right" questions about strategies is far more useful than giving them a to-do list, such as a sensory diet. The Smiths realized that the calming effect Mathias gleaned from doing heavy work during therapy could be partially reproduced by having him help with the grocery shopping. Natalie and Ron also figured out other or strategies, including having Mathias match coupons to items on the grocery shelves (*Task*) and giving him a lollipop to suck on during the shopping trip (*Sensation*). They also discussed the advantages of shopping early in the morning and for much shorter periods of time (*Culture* or *Sensation*) ⟳. As Jamie, Natalie, and Ron worked together, they realized they were not only thinking about *Task*; they were using other elements of A SECRET while they problem-solved.

Find Purposeful Activities That Incorporate "Heavy Work"—Tasks with Proprioceptive Components

As we discussed in the *Sensation* chapter, proprioception is one of the most useful types of sensory input for organizing and calming the nervous system. The "best" proprioceptive input is based on natural "heavy work" activities. The Smiths considered this before they went to the grocery store. How could they give Mathias heavy work activities to help him stay regulated in the over stimulating grocery store environment? They realized that allowing Mathias to be actively involved in the grocery shopping was the perfect way to not only provide sensory input, but actually incorporate many other elements of A SECRET! On the way to the store they talked to Mathias about needing his help with the grocery shopping. This was a shift in the family *Culture* ⟳ . In the past, both parents were so stressed about the outing that they just took turns trying to calm Mathias down. Now, their perspective had shifted. They felt confident and had ideas for how to make this a successful shopping trip! Natalie and Ron knew that they needed to offer choices rather than ask Mathias an open-ended question like "How do you want to help?" or "Mathias, what are you going to do?" Instead, Natalie said, "Okay, Mathias, we are going to need your muscles to help us in the grocery store. Are you going to carry the shopping basket or put the groceries in the shopping cart?" Now, we all know that they didn't need a shopping cart AND a shopping basket, but the point was to give Mathias a job, a *Task*, to give him choices, and opportunities for heavy work.

When they pulled into the parking lot, Natalie and Ron let Mathias climb out of the tall SUV (more heavy work) and close the door (even more heavy work). Then they both knelt down to be on Mathias' eye level. "Okay, team! Who's ready to do some shopping (*Relationship*)? We've got our driver—Mom will push the cart, our organizer—Dad will check the list and cross things off, and our heavy lifter—Mathias will get help with putting food, especially the heaviest things, in the cart!" These very clear instructions and expectations of everyone's role helped Mathias stay organized and know his job (*Task*). "Now, it might be a little loud and bright in the grocery store, so I brought hats to keep the lights out of our eyes, and Mathias' earphones to keep the noise out of your ears. Now we are ready to go! Great, give me a big hug, Mathias!" (See how we fit *Relationship* and *Sensation* in there)! 🔄

Mathias chose to put the groceries in the cart, which provided lots of opportunities for heavy work! In the grocery store, Natalie and Ron had Mathias pick up most of the items on the list or handed them to him to put them in the cart. With his important job, Mathias stayed organized and also stayed engaged with his parents because they were working as a team (*Emotion Regulation*) 🔄. Yes, this took a little bit longer, but not as long as it took to try to calm Mathias down during a meltdown!

A SECRET

Challenge Area	Attunement	Sensation	Emotion Regulation
• Meltdowns during trips to the grocery store	• Pay attention to Mathias' sensory reactions in the grocery store. • Provide support & options when you see his arousal increasing (engine speeding up)	• Provide opportunities for heavy work during grocery shopping • Provide tools to decrease sensory stimuli (e.g., baseball cap and headphones)	• Show excitement about working as a team! • Empathize regarding the loud crowded grocery store • Use calming tools with Mathias

When the Smith family returned to therapy several days later, they not only reported a successful grocery-shopping trip, but they had applied the principles of what they had learned to other circumstances as well. That successful trip to the grocery store was just the beginning of problem-solving how to support Mathias and help him thrive using the elements of A SECRET.

Let's discuss more ideas and process points for incorporating *Task* to daily routines. As always, not all of these suggestions will apply to your child. They also might not fit into your family culture or routines. You decide what fits for your family, and your OT can help you recognize and fit tasks to your child's individual sensory differences.

A SECRET (CONTINUED)

Culture	Relationship	Environment	Task
• Make grocery shopping a fun family team event	• Work as a team • Get down on his level & make eye contact when planning	• Call attention to the hectic environment & the sensory challenge	• Plan simple & fun tasks for Mathias • Offer 2 choices • Include Mathias in planning • Give clear, simple instructions

Assign Daily Chores

Young children enjoy helping out around the house. Many chores require "heavy work," so while helping out at home or at school, children are also getting organizing sensory input (*Sensation*) ⊖. Carrying the laundry basket to the washer or putting away folded sheets and towels is a simple and helpful task that also provides *heavy work* (proprioceptive) input (Figure 11.1). Another excellent activity is gardening (see Figure 11.2). Digging, moving dirt, repotting soil, carrying gardening tools, and helping transplant plants all make good use of muscles and joints and provide great proprioceptive input to calm and organize the nervous system. Washing the car is another example of a task that can provide organizing sensory input (*Sensation*) and might include an opportunity for fun and playful interactions with water (*Relationship*). ⊖

Figure *11.1* A girl carries laundry to her bedroom for heavy work.

Figure *11.2* Planting and gardening can be a helpful proprioceptive activity.

Figure *11.3* Washing a car with an industrial-sized sponge, soap, and water can be a good activity to do before a potentially overstimulating event.

Give some control—offer two choices when possible.

Of course, we know that sometimes our kids don't want to help with chores. They have very little control over their own lives, and many of them (depending on individual differences and developmental levels) are just starting to develop a sense of self. Providing some control over the situation is a great way to build self-awareness and self-esteem. We usually don't want to give open-ended questions ("What do you want to do?" or "Do you want to help?" In this case they might say, "NO!"), but we can offer choices. "You can empty the dishwasher or feed the dog." Remember we're going for a task that will allow your child to be successful. We want this task to be simple and organizing. If we give them a task that is too complex, it may cause more dysregulation. Your OT can help you identify the just-right tasks for your child.

Use Tasks to Provide Structure and Predictability

Create routines

We know that our kids struggle with changes in routine, so we can use predictable or familiar tasks to provide structure and organization in uncertain situations. For example, this may be another time to use a sensory backpack. The backpack stays by the door until it's time to leave the house. But the backpack is the routine! Whenever it's time to leave, especially to go to a new place or to do an unfamiliar activity, the child's job (*Task*) is to get their backpack. Now they are ready to go! But this isn't the only task. Remember that the backpack is filled with familiar and preferred items. Some of these items should be preferred tasks, such as a coloring book and crayons, a book, journal, or a travel puzzle. There are endless options here. What are some of your child's favorite tasks or activities? What can you put in the backpack to keep them occupied and create a sense or routine?

Another example of using *Task* to provide routine might be a simple game that you play as a family. You can play "I Spy" in line at the grocery store or sing "Bingo" in the car, or have your child unwrap several inexpensive "surprise" travel games during airplane rides.

Use visual supports, e.g., picture schedule, visual timer

For homework completion or bedtime routines, a *Time Timer*® can provide helpful visual cues regarding time. The timer pictured in Figure 11.4 shows blocks of time against a colored background. As time passes, the "time timer" shows less and less red. When the red is gone, the time is up. This makes it easier for children to understand the passage of time. It can be used to organize how much time must be devoted to certain tasks at school or at home before the child gets a break and is also useful for myriad other purposes (see *timetimer.com*). Another way to mark the passage of time and set time limits is to use a predetermined number of music tracks.

Figure 11.4 A time timer can help during bedtime routines.

Give clear instructions and limit language

We need to remember that sensory processing challenges may make it difficult to attend to and follow instructions. When asking your child to complete a task, be very clear with instructions. How many steps are they able to complete at a time? For some children, you may have to give one clear instruction at a time.

Limit the amount of language you use when giving instructions. Let's use the bedtime routine as an example. When you want your child to go to their bedroom, put their pajamas on, go to the bathroom, brush their teeth, and pick out a book, you can't say, "Go to your bedroom, put your pajamas on, go to the bathroom, brush your teeth, and pick out a book." You might say, "It's time to put on your pajamas; they are on your bed." Here, you give one verbal instruction, and you also provided a visual support by laying the pajamas out on the bed ahead of time. A verbal cue combined with a visual cue can be very

Time for Bed!

Put on PJs

Brush teeth

Go potty

Find a book

Figure 11.5 Example of a visual schedule for the bedtime routine

helpful for kids who struggle with planning and organizing. Once pajamas are on, you can give the next instruction. If your child still struggles with verbal instructions, this might be a good time to use a visual schedule (Figure 11.5). This way, you can really limit the amount of language your child has to process.

Include playfulness during daily chores or routines

Make a game out of transitions, with a fun goal/motivating concept.
Transitions are difficult for our sensory kids, so the more playful we can be, the better. We worked with a father who would make simple games to transitions from therapy to the car. "Okay, it's time to go. How many steps do you think it is from here to the car?" Or sometimes it was animal walks: "What are you going to be today, an elephant or a kangaroo?" Either way, it was fun; the simple task gave some structure and organization to the transition, and there's a lot of proprioceptive input to boot!

Add stop/go, fast/slow moments and games during chores. This will not only make chores more fun, but you'll also be working on body awareness and self-regulation! We suggest referring to a visual like the engine scale (Figure 11.6).

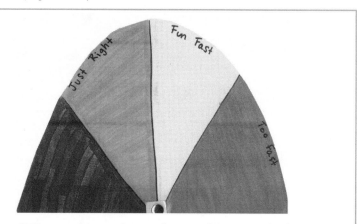

Figure 11.6 We use this engine scale to refer to our bodies as car engines. Our bodies can be slow, just right, fun fast, or too fast. See chapter 8 for more information. Adapted from Williams & Shellenberger, 1996.

Make Sure the Task Provides the Just-Right Challenge

Use calming tasks to develop self-regulation

When we use *Task* to support regulation, it is essential that children are successful. If the point of the task is to slow down your child's engine, it should be familiar and fun. If we choose tasks that are too challenging, we risk frustration and then more dysregulation. This is not the time to challenge your child. Find tasks that are enjoyable for your child and that hold their interest. Now that you can see how the elements of A SECRET flow together, you can also consider tasks that direct support the development of self-regulation. For instance, you could do 10 deep breaths with your child. The deep breathing engages the parasympathetic nervous system (see chapter 3), and the act of counting the 10 breaths provides a simple cognitive challenge that may help to break the cycle of increased arousal or dysregulation.

Simple Tasks for Calming

- Jigsaw puzzle
- Coloring book
- Drawing
- Familiar yoga routine
- Specific breathing exercises
- Reading a book
- Legos®

What familiar tasks or activities are calming for your child? Everyone has their own preferred tasks. Create a list of favorite calming tasks *with* your child.

For children who thrive on change and unpredictability

Some of our sensory kids really love a challenge. They get bored with routines and can easily lose interest in doing the same task or playing the same game over and over. For these kids, we need to think about balancing novel and familiar activities to increase engagement and participation. Sometimes just a slight change in routine can be helpful, but other times you might need a major change. Here are some examples for creating change with structure.

Create Novelty with Tasks

- Post a visual chore schedule and rotate tasks every day
- Schedule a dedicated play time every evening and change the game each day
- Create a family outing wheel with different options for body-based outdoor activities (e.g., walking, bike riding, hopscotch, jumping rope, playing tag)
- Choose a different song to sing each night when clearing the table after dinner
- Provide visuals with specific exercises for sensory breaks from seated schoolwork

Here are some examples of how to translate *Task* strategies to your child's classroom:

- Provide structure by assigning goal-directed tasks, such as wiping down tables, sweeping after snack time, or placing all the chairs onto the desks at the end of the day

- Support attention and engagement in school work by ensuring proper positioning for learning: feet flat on the floor, ankles—knees—hips at 900, work surface at elbow height
- Provide visual schedules for the entire classroom
- Use visual timers to help children stay on task for short periods of time
- Simplify your language when giving instructions
- Provide clear instructions for varied learning preferences
  - Present verbal instructions one at a time
  - Provide clear, written instructions
  - Consider a picture schedule
  - Give an example or demonstration when possible

How Does Dysregulation Affect Task?

When we think about *Task* in A SECRET, we have to consider how this element can challenge some of our kids. We aren't only thinking about strategies to support regulation and success; we are also using this element to recognize individual differences and shift our expectations, especially in certain contexts. In chapter 3, we discussed the science indicating that kids with SPD have different brain connections than neurotypical kids, and different autonomic nervous system functioning. This means they aren't able to calm down as easily or quickly as neurotypical kids. When they are dysregulated or when their arousal levels are high (frustrated, angry, sad, or even happy and excited) they might struggle to complete a task that is easy for them when they are not stressed. In these moments, when our kids are dysregulated, we should not expect them to do what they can do when they are calm, especially if it's a task they're still learning to master. We can provide empathy and validation of feelings (*Emotion Regulation*) while we offer more help with a challenging task.

Example of Adjusting Expectations

Decrease expectations during heightened sensory input or motor challenge

Sally is just learning to tie her shoes. It's been a lot of work for her and her parents because of her difficulty with learning new motor skills (dyspraxia). Sally's parents have been patient and supportive, understanding how Sally's individual sensory differences directly impact her ability to complete this task. Using A SECRET, they taught shoe-tying in the same place every day: a quiet corner in Sally's room (*Environment*) . One parent at a time would help Sally practice the steps of shoe-tying, sitting on the floor with her and playfully celebrating her successes along the way (*Relationship*) . Sally was very proud of herself when she was able to tie both shoes independently! Of course, her parents were also pleased and relived that she was finally independent with this self-care skill. One more thing that would make the morning routine easier!

A few months later, Sally's father, Kia, picked her up from a birthday party. He was feeling stressed because he was facing a deadline at work, the baby was crying after being woken up from a nap in the car, and he knew that traffic would be awful on the way home. Sally was very excited about the birthday party, jumping and spinning, telling her dad about all of the games they played and the party favors she was bringing home! Her engine was definitely running high. Sally didn't want to leave the party and started to get upset when her dad tried to hurry her out the door. Then, of course, it was time to put shoes on. Kia told her very sternly that she needed to be a big girl and put her shoes on. She could tell her dad was frustrated, so she sat down and put her shoes on but started to cry when she couldn't get them tied. Kia could feel his own frustration rising.

"She knows how to tie her shoes," he thought. "Why now, of all times?" Then he remembered all of the things they'd practiced at home and everything they'd learned in OT. Sally's engine was running *too fast*, and he realized that his was, too! Yes, Sally was able to tie her shoes when the environment was quiet and supportive, when her engine was *just right*, and when a parent was there to offer support and co-regulation. Kia was able to catch himself and realize that this was not the time to expect Sally to be independent with tying her shoes and that this was the recipe for a big meltdown. He knelt and smiled at Sally. "Man, my engine is really fast! It's pretty loud in here and it's too noisy for me. Let's get your shoes on and get in the car where it's quiet. I'll help you." Sally still didn't want to leave the party, but Kia knew that things would only escalate if he pushed the shoe-tying in that situation. It was more important to support Sally's regulation in that moment.

Reflection

Take some time to consider the following questions.

What activities or tasks are calming for your child? Do they have games or toys that they prefer when they are stressed?

_____

_____

_____

_____

_____

_____

_____

_____

What games or activities do you enjoy as a family?

_____

_____

_____

_____

_____

_____

_____

What activities or tasks are challenging for your child or family?

_____

_____

_____

_____

_____

_____

_____

_____

_____

How might you change these activities or tasks to support your child?
Or what tools can you add to support emotion regulation when you
have to run errands or transition from one place to another?

_____

_____

_____

_____

_____

_____

_____

_____

References

Williams, M. S., & Shellenberger, S. (1996). *How Does Your Engine Run?: A Leader's Guide to the Alert Program for Self-Regulation*. TherapyWorks, Inc.

On the next page, we provide some examples of *Task* strategies, or what we call process points. These examples will not fit every child or family but should be used as a guide. The reflection above should help you think about tasks that can be used to support your child and your family. Use the reflection to think about *Task* process points that will work for you.

A SECRET

Challenge Area	Attunement	Sensation	Emotion Regulation	Culture	Relationship	Environment	Task
				↻			• Create structure and predictability using visual schedule or timer
		↻					• Create novelty for children who crave change (e.g., new song to sing during transitions, different animal walks each time, new sensory tools in the sensory backpack)
						↻	• Have preferred games or toys available in the car
				↻	↻		• Complete chores as a family or a team
		↻					• Offer calming activity choices with photos of supportive tasks (e.g., breathing exercise, heavy work activity, drawing, puzzle)
			↻				• Add simple cognitive component to transitions (e.g., counting # of steps or performing animal walks to the car)
		↻					• Assign jobs (preferably heavy work) during transitions or outings to crowded places

CHAPTER 12

CASE STUDIES

Lacey

Lacey is a six-year-old in first grade. She is a bright, resilient, imaginative, and playful girl. Lacey is funny and can make others laugh out loud with her wit. She is a fast learner, and her excellent memory is a true strength. She easily generalizes concepts once they are taught to her. In spite of Lacey's intellectual abilities, she struggles academically. The Committee of Special Education has classified Lacey as *Learning Disabled*. Lacey has an Individual Educational Plan (IEP) and receives occupational therapy services twice a week. Lacey gets assistance in reading and in math from a special education teacher who "pushes into" her integrated first grade class.

Unfortunately, Lacey doesn't have many friends. She struggles socially and dislikes school. Lacey avoids her peers. She does not participate during social situations and almost always sits and plays alone during recess and lunch.

Lacey is a favorite of many teachers. In jest, her teachers refer to her as "the one who wears the wrong clothes in all seasons." Her OT, Ana, worked hard on helping her overcome discomfort in wearing certain clothing. Ana collaborated with the school psychologist and classroom teacher, creating a reward system related to wearing the appropriate type of clothing based on weather. Lacey's teacher and Ana created sensory comfort zones in the classroom for Lacey to have a "time-in" place whenever she needed personal space. She has a sensory box filled with fidget and tactile comfort toys, like putty and squishy balls that she keeps in her desk.

Lacey was making great gains in her functioning before the COVID-19 pandemic began. She had started to come to school wearing tights, pants, and long-sleeved blouses. Her responses to fire alarms, loudspeaker announcements, and other unexpected sounds had become increasingly more appropriate. Positive changes in her emotional resilience were noted as she showed more tolerance sitting next to peers, became able to join on the carpet during Read Aloud Time, and became an active participant during music and gym classes. She had far fewer meltdowns and became forgiving if a peer accidentally bumped into her while walking in the hallway. Lacey was beginning to transition more easily to specials and waited patiently for her turn to be called on in class. Lacey had come to terms with allowing all the students in her class to have a turn to answer or ask questions.

Once the pandemic closed her school, children with IEPs, like Lacey, received related services through remote teletherapy.

Let's take a closer look at Lacey's interactions during her teletherapy sessions with her occupational therapist, Ana.

Ana starts the session by saying, "Hi, Lacey. I am so excited to see you online. We will do so many cool things together."

Lacey responds by turning off her video and muting herself. Ana says, "Lacey, I can't see you or hear what you are saying. Don't you want to join me in this session?"

Lacey unmutes her microphone and responds, "No, I don't want to see you or anyone else right now! I want to hang up. I don't like seeing myself on TV. I just want to play with my doll right now."

Ana quickly says, "Okay, Lacey, I understand. This remote connecting is not as much fun as seeing each other live. But I can share my screen with you, and we can play a game. I have a fun app that will allow us to take turns and play. Would that be okay, Lacey? You and your doll can play together on the same team."

Lacey thinks about it for 10 seconds (during which Ana must bite on her tongue to avoid blabbering on), then says, "Maybe. We can talk, but I am not going to show myself online, and that's that!"

Ana allows Lacey to keep her video off during the remote meeting, happy that Lacey has turned her microphone back on and feeling that through interactive play Lacey may start to feel more comfortable and engage more freely. Ana shares her screen with Lacey, and the first activity is tic-tac-toe. Ana has numbered the boxes on the shared tic-tac-toe grid so that she and Lacey can take turns with verbal responses.

Lacey says, "I am the X and you be the O. I go first and I am going to win!"

Ana is satisfied that she has Lacey's attention and focus. "Okay, go ahead and tell me where I should place the first X."

The game takes a few minutes to complete, and Lacey seems to be quite engaged in this cooperative play and, of course, in winning! Ana hopes Lacey will show herself in the next session, but Lacey continues to keep her video off during the next three meetings.

Lacey's mom calls Ana, apologizing for Lacey's behavior. She says, "I am so sorry that Lacey is being disrespectful during your sessions, Ana. She is having such a hard time during this pandemic. She refuses to wear underwear and prefers to walk around practically naked all day! I don't know what to do. All she wants to do is wash her hands a million times a day and hold her doll."

Ana responds, "Please don't apologize. This whole situation is incredibly difficult and confusing for all the children. It is like living in a science fiction movie. And online communication is new and scary."

---

1. Why does Ana talk with Mom alone?

Ana demonstrated her concern for Mom, who doesn't really understand how the pandemic has launched Lacey out of her routine and how the unpredictability has resulted in decreasing Lacey's comfort zone.

Ana understands that different contexts may impact on reactions and behaviors and tries to help Mom understand how challenging the remote learning is for Lacey.

At the same time, speaking to Lacey's mom provides Ana with useful information. After discussing the situation with Lacey's Committee on Special Education (CSE) team, Ana and the psychologist decide to spend some time working with Lacey's mother. Their goal is to further educate Mom about how the pandemic has affected Lacey's emotion regulation issues. They schedule an online session with Mom to help her understand Lacey's needs related to feeling safe and valued.

Ana thinks a lot about how to plan the next remote session. She remembers Lacey talking about how much she loves her doll. Lacey likes to take care of her doll, pretend to feed her, and take care of her beautiful, long hair. Ana decides to try the next online OT session using Lacey's favorite doll. She sends Mom an email with a list of items needed for the next session.

> ### 2. **Why does Ana suggest this activity?**
> Ana has, over time, created a strong bond with Lacey and wants to return to her pre-COVID level of relating and connecting. Thinking that nurturing may impact Lacey's other play skills and fulfill her need for connection, Ana tunes into Lacey mothering her baby doll, taking on the baby's voice when needed for the conversation.

Ana suggests to Mom that she help by explaining to Lacey that the next OT session will be about bathing and caring for her doll. Lacey cheerfully selects the items for her doll's bath. Mom participates in choosing materials too, including a towel, shampoo, thick sponge, hairbrush, and body lotion. Lacey will bathe her doll, use her selected sensory items while bathing the doll, and massage her doll with body lotion. Ana will provide care and comfort to Lacey (and her doll) during this simple sensory motor play.

> **3. How does Ana choose just-right success?**
>
> Ana is aware of the low developmental level of this play activity but feels that Lacey needs a "win" right now, which we call the just-right *success* (rather than the "just-right challenge.")

Ana starts the online session by saying, "Hi, Lacey. I know how much you love your doll and I was wondering if you would like to give her a bubble bath? I would love to share this time with you and your doll."

Much to Ana's surprise, Lacey turns on her video, showing herself to Ana. Lacey is wearing a bathing suit, appropriate for this OT session. Lacey declares, "Yes, I have all of her things ready. My mom is filling the kitchen sink. My doll is really excited for her bubble bath!"

Ana is amazed as she watches Lacey plunge her doll into the sink filled with water. Lacey adds bubble bath to the water, and the doll is embedded in a sea of bubbles. Lacey gets suds all over the sponge. She is scrubbing the doll and squeezing out the sponge using both hands. Lacey smiles and laughs out loud as she continues to engage in this **"heavy work"** play.

What Is Heavy Work?

Heavy work is any type of activity that includes pushing, pulling, lifting, or other "muscle work." Heavy work activities are often used to support kids with sensory processing issues feel centered. Heavy work engages a sense called proprioception and supports body awareness. For children with sensory processing difficulties, learning how to use the sense of proprioception to their advantage through heavy work activities can be especially powerful in helping them pay attention and remain calm in a variety of situations.

Lacey announces, "I am going to wash her hair now! Look how beautiful she looks. She is super clean. I love this."

Ana says, "It looks like you are having a great time, Lacey. Your doll will look even more beautiful when you are all finished."

Lacey does not want to end the session. Ana feels torn but decides to show Lacey how she also wants to stay connected with her during this stressful time in her life. She and Lacey remain on the video call for another 15 minutes, beautifying the doll and talking about what makes baths feel good.

Ana remembers Lacey's first sessions at school and congratulates them both on how far they have come together. Ana says, "Remember what a hard time you had at first when you came to see me at school? It was so hard for you to leave your classroom to go to the OT gym. It's not hard for you anymore. You are getting to be such a big girl! Remember that time when I asked if you wanted to bring a guest from your class to join you, and you responded, 'No! No! Only I will go to your OT room—all by myself!'"

Ana smiles and continues, "Remember when I said, 'Let's go have some fun playing together, Lacey. I will let you choose the first game/ activity that you want. What will it be?' You looked around with wonderment at the great big room; it was full of colorful objects and large, hanging equipment. Then you walked over to the swing and told me that you wanted to play on the swing. You said, 'What is it? It looks like a fishing net!'

"And I replied, 'Sure, Lacey. It's a net and the favorite thing of lots of kids. Climb into the net. You can make up any game you want to. Sometimes kids can figure out how to pretend to be a fish and to make the fish flip out without me touching them. Here we go...' Then I started moving the net swing slowly, gradually building up speed, as you demonstrated enjoyment in the activity."

Ana remembers out loud how Lacey would laugh and giggle during the sensory motor play. She thinks about how Lacey was always eager to engage in activities in the gym that incorporated vestibular and proprioceptive sensations.

---

4. **What is vestibular input used for?**
Vestibular input can be used for a variety of reasons including calming down, increasing focus, and organizing responses, particularly if slow linear movement is used. This speed and intensity results in some therapists nicknaming these "fast/blast" activities.

Lacey is happier after she uses crashing components and feels calmer after climbing up a pole or playing on a large rope attached to the ceiling, which requires sustained effort. It certainly requires creativity to do some of these activities at home!

---

5. How does the activity affect the child?

Proprioception is responsible for helping the body feel where it is in space. Heavy work, as described above, is a strategy used in therapy to target the sense of proprioception. For children with sensory processing difficulties, learning how to use the sense of proprioception to their advantage through heavy work activities can be especially powerful in helping them self-regulate, pay attention, and remain calm in a variety of situations. Does the activity have a lasting effect on the child?

Ana understands how important it is to Lacey to end her sessions feeling calm and hopes it creates a sense of trust between Lacey and herself. Her choice of activities allows Lacey to feel those important emotions at the right time and the right place. This is one of the greatest gifts that OT brings to the team: the ability to understand and bring awareness of the child's sensory and emotional needs.

Let's review some of the lessons we've learned so far during the story about Lacey and Ana.

---

6. How did Ana choose themes for play?

Lacey easily transitioned from being a fish in the net to a mountain climber on a mountain. With developmentally younger play, the theme does not have to be logical, just lots of fantasy with elements combined together. Over time, the themes and organization of the

---

play will increase. In the beginning, it is just important for children to be allowed to "just" play and get used to creating stories.

Ana used stickers to mark each time Lacey made it to the mountaintop. This was not a reward as used in Applied Behavioral Analysis (ABA), but rather a way to keep track of Lacey's progress from 1 to 2 to 3 to eventually 5 mountaintops conquered in one session.

At the end of the session, Lacey would say,

"Ana, I want to stay here all day. I love it here!"

Ana would acknowledge how much fun they had and combine another fun activity with a story and turn the session from having a focus on leaving to planning how to carry it on the next session.

"Lacey, we really did have fun here in the OT room. I have an idea. I bet you've never had a chance to pull through the halls on your tummy at school. Here's a scooter board; as long as you are in OT, we can go back to class using the scooter board to get there. What kind of animal do you want to pretend you are being?"

"How about a turtle?" replied Lacey.

"Great idea!" exclaimed Ana. "How can we continue this game in our next session so that it stays really fun?"

"I have an idea." replied Lacey. "So instead of just a few animals, let's make a whole zoo with everything in the OT room that can be an animal or a fish. Let's make every net, every rope and everything into something that we can pretend an animal would like!"

"Really great idea," replied Ana, "and look, we are back at your classroom. You think about what animals we can be next time and we'll put it together, both of us, okay?" Lacey jumped up off the scooter board and said, "I'm going to slither back into class like a snake so no one will see me. Bye!"

> **7. How did Ana make therapy fun?**
>
> Thereafter, Lacey would sit or lie prone on the scooter and use her arms or legs to propel herself back to class. And her own imagination made it fun. For Lacey, ending her session in this way always made it fun. It was fun for Ana too. Lacey became a special client for Ana, teaching Ana how to combine sensory input with imagination.

Every day together, they explored a new idea; once it was the Amazon River and the jungle, another time it was China and the Great Wall, and yet another day they went to the Empire State Building on the pretend subway (with all activities suspended off the floor so it was tricky indeed!) They went "everywhere together," and Ana snuck in all the sensory input Lacey needed, while Lacey's expectations for herself were kept reasonable by Ana. For example, one day Lacey thought it would be fun to be an eagle and soar to the top of Mt. Everest, which she had just heard of. The goal was always for Lacey to experience success and joy. Ana had to make sure Lacey was considering how to be reasonable and safe with all the play (just like she would need to do in real life). Lacey got the be an eagle, and Ana helped her fly over the mountain.

> **8. How did Ana be creative and experience joy through success?**
>
> Imagine the creativity that went on during these sessions. The themes were great and engaging for both Lacey and Ana during their sessions together. Lacey really was an instructor for Ana, and Ana kept track of all her lessons in her journal. She also used her jour-

nal to keep track of their exciting ideas and trips, and helped Lacey organize the experiences into a "whole," which had lots of academic relevance. There were opportunities for counting, multiplying, and using numbers in all sorts of ways. There were things that needed neat labels in Lacey's best handwriting, and there were even times to talk about some simple science principles! Both Ana and Lacey got an opportunity to grow.

What really makes the kids we see feel good (joyful), less challenged (successful), and less threatened (safe)?

Think about all the hard work that both Ana and Lacey did together. Ana spent a great deal of time with Lacey helping her feel safe, and a side benefit was that Lacey began to really trust Ana. She knew that no matter how big the idea was that she brought in, Ana would join in and help her plan a safe sequence of really fun, safe, and exciting adventures. The other kids did not make fun of Lacey's OT sessions. When they heard about the fun Lacey had, they were jealous!

Lacey felt empowered. Lacey loved playing Twister, playing at the rice table, using Theraputty and hiding coins, using slime, finger-painting and roleplaying. Lacey loved to pretend to be the "captain" of the ship and announce the plan she had for the voyage that she and Ana were about in engage in. Ana learned that Lacey needed to feel in control. She always included Lacey in the planning of the session with appropriate modifications for safety as needed. The time was not spent alone by Ana ahead of time. The planning and thinking was part of the process of the OT sessions. The joint effort they made sealed the bond and enhanced the relationship between Ana and Lacey.

Now, back to the challenge of taking the OT to Lacey at home...

It was the regression from the fairly high level of play down to only having the capacity to carry a baby doll around that had Ana stumped at first. During the teletherapy session, given enough time and space and going at her own rate, Lacey finally made a breakthrough. She started screen sharing, conversing, and experiencing much joy... *joie de vivre*. That's the secret!

In the next online teletherapy session, Ana plans to have Mom and Lacey work together. She plans on the phone with Lacey's mom at a time Lacey is not at home. Together they plan a session in which Mom and Lacey will create glueless slime. Ana sends the fluffy slime recipe to Mom and a video of steps required to make the slime.

Ana thinks this will be fun for both Mom and Lacey. Mom sends Ana multiple texts throughout the day telling her how excited Lacey is to make the slime. Finally, when it is time for the remote session to begin, Ana says, "Lacey, Mom and I talked, and we thought you and Mom would have fun making slime together. How does that sound? Once it is made, you can build together and create whatever you would like."

Ana calls Lacey and says, "This is what we will use to make our slime, and Mom, why don't you get a copy of the recipe so it's handy?"

Mom gets the card with the recipe on it. Ana continues to read out loud, and each step is accomplished before the next step is read.

Lacey gives Ana a thumbs up and says ,"Mom, let's do this together, okay?"

Ana says to Lacey, "Okay, let's start by putting in the cornstarch, Lacey. We need ¼ of a cup to be put inside a bowl. Put ½ cup shampoo and ¼ cup of cornstarch in a bowl."

Ana detects the excitement in both Lacey and Mom. They are cohesive and working together. Both Mom and Lacey seem thrilled. Mom jumps in and says, "Lacey, is it okay if I pour the cornstarch into the measuring cup?"

Lacey says, "Yes, Mom, you be the one who measures all the stuff, and I'll be the one who gets to mix it all up together!

"Great!" Mom says.

1. Mix well.
2. Add 3 drops of food coloring.
3. Add 1 tablespoon of water and stir.
4. Slowly add 5 more tablespoons of water, stirring well after each one.
5. Knead the slime for about 5 minutes.

The process of measuring and mixing all the ingredients together is working even better than Ana thought it would. Lacey is considerate and cooperative. She loves the experience of putting her hands into the bowl and squeezing, mashing, and mixing all the ingredients together.

Once again, we see *joie de vivre* for both Lacey and Mom during this activity. This activity is loaded with tactile, visual, and proprioceptive sensations! This is just what Lacey needs to be organized, but it is easy

enough to guarantee success! In addition, it helps with tactile discrimination.

---

9. What is tactile discrimination?

The tactile system is critical in helping children motor plan and
learn the differences in qualities of various sensory features. Lacey
learns how much force and pressure is needed to get all these ingredients to blend. These are aspects of math, reading and many other
higher level abilities that are all part of this activity.

Sensory discrimination refers to the process whereby specific
qualities of **sensory** stimuli are perceived and meaning attributed to them. The process of discrimination refers to comparing the
quantitative and qualitative attributes of one stimulus to another
stimulus.

After all the ingredients are mixed, Ana says, "Wow, what a great job
you both did! Now you can decide what to create out of the slime."

Mom jumps in. "Lacey, can we make caves and create some animals
out of the slime?"

Lacey smiles and nods.

This was a great session for both Mom and Lacey. Both experienced
an array of sensory inputs, worked together, followed sequenced steps,
and created and enacted a final plan.

Ana says, "Just think of all the baking activities that you can both do
together. I bet you could make the best cookies ever."

Lacey is gently recommending additional sensory-based activities
in which Mom and Lacey can engage and enjoy each other's company
while succeeding at a functional task.

> **10. What did Mom contribute?**
>
> Ana's idea to include Mom in this session was perfect. Mom had been expressing feelings of helplessness due partly to the pandemic and partly to her continued struggle to be the "perfect mom" and help Lacey all the time.

Lacey nods and says, "Yay! Mom, every week can we make something together? I would really like that."

Mom replies, "Me too, Lacey."

Lacey gives Mom a big hug and says, "Thanks, Mom. This is really great!"

Ana knows how great Lacey's words feel to Mom. Ana chose the "just-right success" through an activity that brought them together in harmony in spite of the pandemic.

Questions to Our Readers:

Let's think of questions that will help us understand Lacey's and Mom's feelings and responses:

1. What was the turning point for Lacey in this story? What helped her emotional reactions become positive during teletherapy?

2. With which sensory experiences did Lacey engage most and why?

3. Which activities provided the most supportive connecting time for Lacey?

4. What aspects of the session provided Lacey with the "just-right success?"

5. What happened to Lacey's emotional state when Mom joined the session?

6. What helped Lacey participate in the video sessions?

These are just examples of some of the questions raised when trying to understand our children and their reactions. Now, let's think about Ana's journey through this telemedicine experience.

1. How did Ana feel before the first session?

2. What did she do when Lacey refused to turn on her video in the first session?

3. Did it seem like Ana was on the right track?

4. Why do you think she turned to using Lacey's doll as a prompt? Did that help Lacey?

5. What more could she have done along these lines instead of moving on to a new project, making slime?

6. Through Ana's work with Lacey, she was aware of what sensory experiences helped Lacey feel more comfortable during the bath time activity. How did the "heavy work" sensations of pushing, squeezing, pulling and kneading affect Lacey and why?

7. Ana knows that the sensory experiences offered during the session with Lacey were not the main reason for Lacey's turnaround during the teletherapy sessions. Sensory tools are a means to an end, and the end is creating enduring relationships that embody

success and joy. What sensations contributed to Lacey's sense of accomplishment?

8. What are some other activities you think would be at the just-right level for Lacey and Mom?

Ana understood that Lacey was feeling out of control because of the teletherapy required due to pandemic conditions. Lacey communicated her discomfort by turning her camera and video off, signaling to Ana that she needed help.

Ana chose the "just-right success" for all sessions. She knew that decreasing the developmental expectations of the activity would tend to keep Lacey's emotions controlled. All sessions were filled with fun! Much of the fun came from the sensory opportunities offered. She understands that her relationship with Lacey was developed over time, the trusting bond being earned through their weeks of work together. Some of the sensory programs that were set up at school were continued at home, with Mom working collaboratively with Lacey. These were all critical features of understanding Lacey to cope and stay regulated under the difficult conditions of the pandemic.

Sometimes when kids are exposed to specific media like video chatting, some desensitization occurs after a period time. Once Lacey got the hang of the teletherapy, she did become more comfortable with it.

9. Which do you think is a better approach and why?

Perhaps as practicing OTs, it would be best to expose our clients to both live and video chatting sessions. One thing learned from this pandemic is how so many of our children may do fairly well in a school environment yet easily fall apart in a different context, like video chats.

10. What elements of school are most regulating for our kids? Which elements of the school day are just too challenging for most kids to get comfortable with?

11. What lesson can you take away from this vignette?

12. What was unique about Ana's role? How did Ana get the most out of her sessions with Lacey? How would you feel keeping a journal and following in private the thoughts that were enhanced compared with the additional stress you might feel with this type of new experience?

Luke

This case study is an example of A SECRET in action. It is one family's story of how they learned to use A SECRET to support Luke (and the entire family) and create strategies for any situation.

When Luke was five years old, his parents were at their wits' end. They recognized Luke's sensory differences and requested an OT referral from their pediatrician. His parents were struggling with Luke's frequent and intense meltdowns and reported severe emotional reactivity, anxiety, an extremely limited diet, challenges with peer relationships, and heightened sensory reactivity. At points, they described "being held hostage" by Luke's behaviors, unable to leave the house or enjoy family get-togethers. Luke's challenges with self-regulation and sensory processing were greatly impacting family life and increasing stress levels for Luke, his parents, and his older brother.

Luke's initial OT assessment revealed many strengths, starting with the amazing support of his family and their strong relationships. Luke immediately demonstrated a passion for moving, labeling himself a movementalist! He was a bright and curious little boy with a wonderful sense of humor and a strong interest in science and in learning about his body. Along with his many strengths, the OT assessment showed challenges with vestibular and proprioceptive processing, which contributed to decreased body awareness and heightened anxiety. Sensory over-responsivity affected his ability to self-regulate and organize his parasympathetic (calming) nervous system, and he demonstrated difficulty with planning new motor sequences or movements.

Early in the OT process, Luke and his parents learned to recognize and pay attention to his sensory differences and changes in his arousal level, referring to his body as a car engine and identifying when he was slow, just right, fun-fast, or too fast.

Figure 12.1

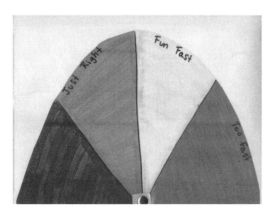

Figure 12.1 Using the Engine Scale (adapted from Williams & Shellenberger 1996), children can learn to recognize and attune to changes in their arousal levels, from slow (tired, sleepy), just right (alert and ready to engage), fun-fast (moving, playing associated with emotions of happy, excited, surprised, etc.), to too fast (associated with emotions of angry, upset, mad, sad, frustrated, etc.)

He began to refer to his amygdala and cerebral cortex, understanding for the first time that he could learn to have some control by using his thinking brain. Luke's parents attended OT sessions and learned how to support his complex sensory and regulatory challenges. They learned to read his triggers and began thinking about how to use his strengths to support his challenge areas.

With this foundation set, Luke's OT decided to introduce A SECRET. It was time for Luke and his family to start problem-solving their own solutions. For this family, the OT's tools and strategies were no longer A SECRET! Using the categories of A SECRET, Luke and his family began to identify ways they could create supports using sensory tools, relationships, environmental changes, and calming tasks. They learned how to encourage attention and emotion regulation. Most importantly, with repetition and practice, they began to weave these tools into their daily routines and shift their family culture.

Through the process of using and learning A SECRET, Luke's parents started to recognize how important it was for them to take care of themselves. When they were able to stay calm and regulated, Luke was more successful staying calm and regulated. Practicing their own self-care, Luke's parents were also able to model self-regulation tools for him. They recognized and internalized the crucial need to use co-regulation strategies to help Luke begin the long process of learning emotion regulation strategies.

Luke and his family did not grasp the concept of A SECRET imme-diately, but they did learn tools along the way to support themselves. With practice and repetition, they began to initiate their own strategies and continued to come to their OT for support with different challenge areas or challenging situations. Luke, his parents, and his OT would use A SECRET to discuss challenges, highlight Luke's strengths, and prob-lem-solve individualized support plans.

Figure 12.2

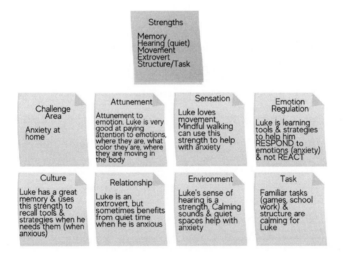

Figure 12.2 This is an example of A SECRET that Luke created with his OT and his mom to support his anxiety at home—an area of challenge that he identified.

Years later, Luke and his parents continue to use A SECRET as they navigate adolescence. They recognize potentially challenging situations before they occur and use A SECRET to plan and prepare together. Luke's father reports that they "use A SECRET to rehearse potential situations and then refer back to it during short-term events." They feel empowered as a family, knowing that they "are on the same page and have a short-term integrated action plan."

For Luke's parents, A SECRET has been essential in helping them recognize that nobody's done anything wrong when they hit a rough patch. As Luke's father said, they recognize that a reaction "is symptomatic of some sensory issues, and rather than trying to succumb to a fight or flight response, there's a larger set of tools that you can use to intervene and hopefully create another layer of pause to be able to start doing some problem-solving for nervous systems to organize, amygdalas to calm down, and co-regulation to occur."

Luke's mother reports that he "has gained more confidence and more trust that the next time, he'll be able to handle a situation and have more ways to cope." According to his parents, "he has learned to trust himself more and to be able to handle unexpected situations." They have learned to trust Luke's ability to regulate.

For Luke's family, A SECRET has been a life changer. It has very literally changed the family culture. "It's woven into our whole fabric."

The next page shows an example of Luke's A SECRET.

A SECRET

Challenge Area	Attunement	Sensation	Emotion Regulation

• Overnight Camp	• Recognize when your arousal is high:
	
	  * Use safe word – "JUMPS"
	
	  * Handy brain model
		• Stretchy band for proprioception
		
		• Rubber band on wrist to bring you back to your body
		
		• Jumps for proprioception and calming
			• Use pre-frontal cortex (willful control) to hold it together until you're in a safe space
			
			• Mindfulness to support amygdala growth

A SECRET *(CONTINUED)*

Culture	Relationship	Environment	Task

• Supports:
 	
  * Use all other tools in A SECRET to support challenges
 	
  * Create a plan for food
 	
• Challenges:
 	
  * Temperature
 	
  * Camping
 	
  * Loud, crowded environment
 	
  * Food
	• Allies:
	
	  * You and your mom are each other's person
	
	  * Trust and take care of each other
		• Doctor's prescription: Airbnb or hotel
		
		• Script: "I'm going to stay nearby because camping maxes me out!"
			• 10 Jumps
			
			• Simple cognitive & whole-body task to reset your amygdala

References

Williams, M. S., & Shellenberger, S. (1996). *How Does Your Engine Run?: A Leader's Guide to the Alert Program for Self-Regulation.* TherapyWorks, Inc.

Print

Ready ... Set ... R.E.L.A.X.: A Research-Based Program of Relaxation, Learning, and Self-Esteem for Children by Jeffrey S. Allen, M.Ed. and Roger J. Klein, Psy.D.

The Incredible 5-Point Scale: The Significantly Improved and Expanded Second Edition; Assisting Students in Understanding Social Interactions and Controlling their Emotional Responses by Kari Dunn Buron and Mitzi Curtis

When My Worries Get Too Big! by Kari Dunn Buron

Yoga Calm for Children by Lynea Gillen and James Gillen

The Resilient Parent by Mantu Joshi

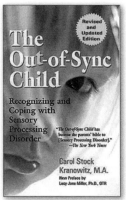

The Out-of-Sync Child by Carol Stock Kranowitz, M.A.

The Out-of-Sync Child Has Fun by Carol Stock Kranowitz, M.A.

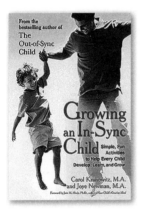

Growing an In-Sync Child by Carol Stock Kranowitz, M.A. and Joye Newman

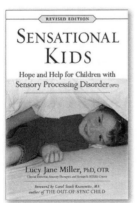

Sensational Kids by Lucy Jane Miller, PhD, OTR

Sensitive Sam: Sam's Sensory Adventure Has a Happy Ending! by Marla Roth-Fisch

The Whole-Brain Child Workbook: Practical Exercises, Worksheets and Activities to Nurture Developing Minds by Daniel Siegel and Tina Payne Bryson

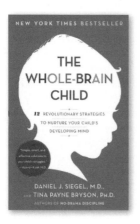

The Whole-Brain Child: 12 Revolutionary Strategies to Nurture Your Child's Developing Mind by Daniel Siegel and Tina Payne Bryson

The Time-In Tool Kit by Suzanne Tucker

Online

STAR Institute

https://sensoryhealth.org

Hand in Hand Parenting

https://www.handinhandparenting.org

SI Network

http://sinetwork.org

SPD Resource Center

https://www.sensory-processing-disorder.com

REFERENCES

Ahn R.R., Miller L.J., Milberger, S., & McIntosh, D.N. (2004). Prevalence of parents' perceptions of sensory processing disorders among kindergarten children. *American Journal of Occupational Therapy, 58*(3), 287-302.

Ben-Sasson, A., Carter, A.S., & Briggs-Gowan, M.J. Sensory over-responsivity in elementary school: prevalence and social-emotional correlates. (2009). *Journal of Abnormal Child Psychology, 37,* 705-716.

Blair, C., & Razza, R.P. (2007). Relating effortful control, executive function, and false belief understanding to emerging math and literacy ability in kindergarten. *Child Development, 78*(2), 647-663.

Bornstein, B.H., Neely, C.B., & LeCompte, D.C. (1995). Visual distinctiveness can enhance recency effects. *Memory & Cognition, 23*(3), 273-278.

Burleigh, J.M., McInstosh, K.W., & Thompson, M.W. (2001). Central auditory processing disorders. In Bundy, A., Lane, S.J., Murray, E. (Eds.,) *Sensory Integration: Theory and Practice* (2nd ed., pp. 141-165). F.A. Davis, Co.

Cameron, O.G. (2001). Interoception: the inside story—a model for psychosomatic processes. *Psychosomatic Medicine, 63*(5), 697-710.

Chudler, E.H. *Neuroscience for Kids.* http://faculty.washington.edu/chudler/neurok.html. Accessed May 19, 2011.

Cross, K.P. (2005). *Collaborative Learning Techniques: A Handbook for College Faculty.* Josse-Bass.

Dunn, W., & Brown, C. (1997). Factor analysis on the Sensory Profile from a national sample of children without disabilities. *American Journal of Occupational Therapy, 51*(7), 490-495.

Dunn, W. (2001). The sensations of everyday life: empirical, theoretical and pragmatic considerations. *American Journal of Occupational Therapy, 55*(6), 608-620.

Eisenberg, N., Cumberland, A., & Spinrad, T.L. (1998). Parental socialization of emotion. *Psychological Inquiry, 9*(4), 241-273.

Eisenberg, N., Hofer, C., & Vaughan, J. (2007). Effortful control and its socioemotional consequences. In Gross, JJ, (Ed.), *Handbook of Emotion Regulation*, (pp. 287-306). Guilford Press.

Goldsmith, H.H., Van Hulle, C.A., Arneson, C.L., Schreiber, J.E., & Gernsbacher, M.A. (2006). A population-based twin study of parentally reported tactile and auditory defensiveness in young children. *Journal of Abnormal Child Psychology, 34*(3), 393–407.

Gross, J.J. (1998). Antecedent- and response-focused emotion regulation: divergent consequences for experience, expression, and physiology. *Journal of Personality and Social Psychology, 74*(1), 224-237.

James, K., Miller, L.J., Schaaf, R., Nielsen, D.M., & Schoen, S.A. (2001). Phenotypes within sensory modulation dysfunction. *Comprehensive Psychiatry.* http://www.elsevier.com/wps/find/ journaldescription.cws_home/623360/description.

REFERENCES

Jin, E.W., & Shevell, S.K. (1996). Color memory and color constancy. *Journal of the Optical Society of America. A. Optics, image science, and vision, 13*(10), 1981-1991.

Johnson, D.J., Jaeger, E., Randolph, S.M., Cauce, A.M., Ward, J., & the NICHD Early Child Care Research Network. (2003). Studying the effects of early child care experiences on the development of children of color in the United States: Toward a more inclusive research agenda. *Child Development, 74*(5), 1227-1244.

Johnson, K. (1998). The effects of six colors on teenage mood states. KJ Research. www.inmind.com/schools/CVGS/sturesearch/Johnson/.

Law, M.B., Pratt, J., & Abrams, R.A. (1995). Color-based inhibition of return. *Perception & Psychophysics, 57*(3), 402-408.

McIntosh, D.N., Miller, L.J., Shyu, V., & Hagerman, R.J. (1999). Sensory-modulation disruption, electrodermal responses, and functional behaviors. *Developmental Medicine & Child Neurology, 41*(9), 608-615.

Lewit, E.M., & Baker, L.S. (1995). School readiness. *Future Child, 5*(2), 128-139.

Lindberg, J.A., & Swick, A.M. (2002). *Common-sense classroom management: surviving September and beyond in the elementary classroom.* Corwin Press.

May-Benson, T.A., Koomar, J.A., & Teasdale, A. (2009). Incidence of pre-, peri-, and post-natal birth and developmental problems of children with sensory processing disorder and children with autism spectrum disorder. *Frontiers Integrative Neuroscience, 3*(31), 1-12.

McIntosh, D.N., Miller, L.J., Shyu, V., & Hagerman, R.J. (1999). Sensory-modulation disruption, electrodermal responses, and functional behaviors. *Developmental Medicine & Child Neurology, 41*(9), 608-615.

Miller, L.J. (2006). *Sensational Kids: Hope and Help for Children with Sensory Processing Disorder*. Penguin Group.

Miller, L.J., Anzalone, M.E., Lane, S.J., Cermak, S.A., & Osten, E.T. (2007). Concept evolution in sensory integration: a proposed nosology for diagnosis. *American Journal of Occupational Therapy, 61*(2), 135-140.

Miller, L.J., Cermak, S., Lane, S., Anazalone, M., & Koomar, J.. (2004). Defining sensory processing disorder and its subtypes: position statement on terminology related to sensory integration dysfunction. *SI Focus*, 6-8.

Miller, L.J., Coll, J.R., & Schoen, S.A. (2007). A randomized controlled pilot study of the effectiveness of occupational therapy for children with sensory modulation disorder. *American Journal of Occupational Therapy, 61*(2), 228-238.

Miller, L.J., Lane, S.J., Cermak, S.A., Anzalone, M., & Osten, B. (2005). Regulatory-sensory processing disorders in children. In Greenspan, S.I., Wieder, S. (Eds.), *Diagnostic Manual for Infancy and Early Childhood: Mental Health, Developmental, Regulatory-Sensory Processing, Language and Learning Disorders* (pp. 73-112). Interdisciplinary Council on Developmental and Learning Disorders.

REFERENCES

Ognibene, T.C. (2002). Distinguishing sensory modulation dysfunction from attention- deficit/hyperactivity disorder: sensory habituation and response inhibition processes [dissertation]. University of Denver.

Radeloff, D.J. (1990). Role of color in perception of attractiveness. *Perceptual and Motor Skills, 71*(1), 151-160.

Schneider, M.L., Moore, C.F., Gajewski, L.L., Larson, J.A., Roberts, A.D., Converse, A.K., & Dejesus, O.T. (2008). Sensory processing disorder in a primate model: evidence from a longitudinal study of prenatal alcohol and prenatal stress effects. *Child Development, 79*(1), 100-113.

Shoda, Y., Mischel, W., & Peake, P.K. (1990). Preschool delay of gratification: Identifying diagnostic conditions. *Developmental Psychology, 26,* 978-986.

Shonkoff, J.P., & Phillips, D.A. (2000). *From Neurons to Neighbourhoods: The Science of Early Childhood Development.* National Academy Press.

Terwogt, M.M., & Hoeksma, J.B. (1995). Colors and emotions: preferences and combinations. *The Journal of General Psychology, 122*(1), 5-17.

Underhill, P. (2000). *Why We Buy: The Science of Shopping.* Simon and Schuster.

Walker, M. (1991). *The Power of Color.* Avery Publishing Group.

Williams, B.R., Ponesse, J.S., Schachar, R.J., Logan, G.D., & Tannock, R. (1999). Development of inhibitory control across the life-span. *Developmental Psychology, 35,* 205–213.

AUTHORS

 **Dr. Lucy Miller** has been investigating, analyzing, and explaining Sensory Processing Disorder (SPD) to other scientists, professionals, and parents since she studied under sensory integration pioneer A. Jean Ayres, Ph.D., more than 30 years ago. Since then, studies by Dr. Miller and her colleagues have helped bring SPD widespread recognition, and her work with families has improved countless lives. Thanks specifically to Dr. Miller's mobilization of the research community, SPD now appears in two diagnostic manuals: the ICDL's *Diagnostic Manual for Infancy and Early Childhood* and *The Diagnostic Classification: Zero to Three*. Her application has led to consideration of SPD for inclusion in the 2013 revision of the *Diagnostic and Statistical Manual* (DSM-V). Dr. Miller has also developed seven nationally standardized tests for use worldwide to assess and diagnose SPD and other developmental disorders and delays. Dr. Miller has been featured on NBC's *The Today Show* and ABC's *20/20*, in *The New York Times*, and in numerous other popular and professional publications. She is the author of more than 60 articles and/or chapters in scientific and professional journals, magazines, and textbooks and is a frequent presenter or speaker at conferences and workshops worldwide. She has received more than 30 funded awards and grants to further research on SPD and other childhood disabilities. In 2004, Dr. Miller received the Award of Merit from the American Occupational Therapy Association, the profession's highest honor. In 2005, she was awarded the Martin Luther King, Jr. Humanitarian Award by the state of Colorado.

 **Dr. Lisa Porter** is an occupational therapist, mentor, professor, and author. She received her master's degree in Occupational Therapy from Rockhurst University in 1994, a doctorate in Occupational Therapy from Rocky Mountain University of Health Professions in 2017, and a PhD in Pediatric Science in 2020. She has a wide range of clinical experience spanning three decades and specializes in the assessment and treatment of individuals with sensory processing and integration challenges.

Dr. Porter's the founder and director of Sensory KIDS in Portland, Oregon. She is a faculty member of STAR Institute in Colorado, where she travels frequently to mentor experienced therapists. She specializes in sensory and relationship-based therapy and holds certifications in Sensory Integration, DIR/Floortime, and Yoga Calm. Lisa has advanced training in the SOS Feeding Approach, Integrated Listening Systems, and Interpersonal Neurobiology. She is passionate about learning, mentoring, listening to families' stories, and playing!

Dr. Porter's current research focuses on parent education, using A SECRET to support families living with sensory and regulatory challenges. The findings from her mixed-methods study are integrated into this edition of *No Longer A SECRET*. She is continuing this line of research, giving voice to parents' experiences, and incorporating their stories into clinical practice and education. When she is not working, Lisa enjoys traveling, backpacking, kayaking, reading, and cooking—along with finding new ways to support her own sensory lifestyle!

Dr. Doreit Bialer is an experienced seminar leader and educational adjunct instructor who has lectured and provided numerous clinical workshops on Sensory Processing Disorder, Handwriting, Motor Learning, Pediatrics, and School-Based Therapy. She has been an independent provider and consultant to school districts and preschools and is an active member of the American Occupational Therapy Association. Dr. Bialer provides Professional Development Workshops to a number of teachers sharing her knowledge. Dr. Bialer is a Certified Handwriting Instructor who consults with multiple teachers to assist in teaching the elements of handwriting.

Dr. Bialer is a graduate of New York University, where she received her B.S. and Advanced Master's Degree in Occupational Therapy. She completed her post-professional doctorate in occupational therapy from Rocky Mountain University in the area of Pediatric Science. Dr. Bialer holds certifications in Neurodevelopmental Therapy in both Pediatrics and Adults and in the Administrations and Interpretation of the Sensory Integration and Praxis Tests. Dr. Bialer is a certified Pilates Mat Instructor and holds a Personal Training Certification from Hofstra University Academy of Applied Personal Training Education (AAPTE). She co-authored a book with Dr. Lucy J. Miller and the Star Center called *No Longer A SECRET: Unique Common-Sense Strategies for Children with Sensory and Motor Challenges.*

Dr. Bialer is an Advanced Mentored Clinician in Sensory Processing Disorder. She studied under the guidance of Dr. Lucy J Miller and Dr. Sarah Shoen and continues to work closely as a consultant and independent provider to multiple preschools, school districts, and private schools. Dr. Bialer is a private practitioner working in a state-of-the-art sensory gym who dedicates her professional life to working with children and families. As an evidence-based practitioner, her goal is help children and families successfully function and participate in the home and school and within the community.